YOU NEED TO MEMORIZE
SCRIPTURE

D1112936

YOU NEED TO
MEMORIZE
SCRIPTURE

By

N. A. Woychuk, M.A., Th.D.

Author, forty three memory books for all age levels,
numerous other books and Bible games.

Foreword by

Dr. Kenneth G. Hanna

Scripture Memory Fellowship International

P.O. Box 411551, St. Louis, MO 63141 • 314/ 569-0244

iv

You Need to Memorize Scripture

© 1993 by N. A. Woychuk

ISBN 1-880960-01-X

Library of Congress Catalog Card Number 92-091188

Cover by Glenn Myers © 1993

Inside art illustrations by J. Emerson Russell, M.A., Th.M.

Printed in the United States of America

Affectionately dedicated
to
Rev. Andrew E. Hamilton,
a faithful friend, a wise counsellor,
a brother beloved,
and to
James A. Woychuk, my dear son.
His keen delight in the Scriptures and his
sincere desire to be a "doer of the word,"
are indeed a worthy illustration
of the message in this book.

God's Unchanging Word

For feelings come and feelings go,
And feelings are deceiving;
My warrant is the Word of God,
Naught else is worth believing.

Though all my heart should feel condemned
For want of some sweet token,
There is One greater than my heart
Whose Word cannot be broken.

I'll trust in God's unchanging Word
Till soul and body sever;
For, though all things shall pass away,
His Word shall stand forever.

—Martin Luther

Contents

CHAPTER   PAGE

1 - NEED 1

2 - MEMORY 5

3 - WHY 11

4 - INTEREST 19

5 - PLAN 24

6 - INCENTIVES 31

7 - EXAMPLES 41

8 - CHILDREN 53

9 - UNDERSTANDING 66

10 - CONCENTRATION 70

11 - STRATEGIES 76

12 - MNEMONICS 83

13 - PRESSURES 88

14 - FORGETTING 97

15 - MEDITATING 101

16 - APPROPRIATING 110

17 - ABIDING 130

18 - OVERFLOWING 137

19 - TRANSLATIONS 143

Century follows century—
    There it stands.
Empires rise and fall and are forgotten—
    There it stands.
Dynasty succeeds dynasty—
    There it stands.
Kings are crowned and uncrowned—
    There it stands.
Despised and torn to pieces—
    There it stands.
Storms of hate swirl about it—
    There it stands.
Atheists rail against it—
    There it stands.
Agnostics smile cynically—
    There it stands.
Profane punsters caricature it—
    There it stands.
Unbelief abandons it—
    There it stands.
Higher critics deny its inspiration—
    There it stands.
An anvil that has broken a million hammers—
    There it stands.
The flames are kindled about it—
    There it stands.
Radicalism rants and raves against it—
    There it stands.
Fogs of sophistry conceal it temporarily—
    There it stands.
The tooth of time gnaws but makes no dent in it—
    There it stands.
Infidels predict its abandonment—
    There it stands.
Modernism tries to explain it away—
    There It Stands!
                      —A. Z. Conrad

Foreword

Dr. Woychuk has rendered a valuable service to all who love the Scriptures (and to those who don't, but should). He has distilled a lifetime of experience in Scripture memorization into one practical, easy to read volume. Over one million people have already found help through his program. This volume will open the rewarding world of Scripture memorization to a whole new generation and encourage those already involved.

Like Dr. Woychuk, my childhood was spent in Western Canada and I was introduced to Scripture memorization as a teenager. Summer camp, a Sunday School class, and the Bible all worked together to bring me to Christ. I went to Sunday School, hoping to learn more about the Bible and become eligible for the Summer Bible Camp. Pastor Douglas Stimers, my Sunday School teacher, also gave me a booklet containing a list of appropriate Scripture references. He encouraged me to start memorizing. I did, with enthusiasm.

Our memory is like a bank. It is a treasure house from which we may draw in times of need. What we draw from it depends on what we have deposited in it. The larger and more worthy the investment, the greater and more valuable the resource available.

The earlier you start and the more often you deposit Scripture in your memory bank, the greater your dividend will be. But, it's never too late to start. This practical volume will motivate you to get started and will show you how to do it. It's a how-to-do-it book that is a delight to read.

These pages will provide that much needed motivation, which is a common problem. They will also address, in a very practical way, how to do it. The place of incentives, the importance of accountability and repetition and other important elements are simply but carefully discussed.

Dr. Woychuk has devoted a lifetime to helping people discover the benefits of Scripture memorization. This book captures all that insight and invites you to share in the profit and the pleasure. Read it and do it today!

Dr. Kenneth G. Hanna,
President
Bryan College
January 25, 1993   Dayton, Tennessee

Preface

This may well be the first book that you are reading on Memorizing Scripture because few books on the subject have ever been written.

I was born and reared in a rural area, seventy miles north of Winnipeg, Canada. In the good providence of God, I memorized five hundred Bible verses in my early teens. I did not understand them, nor did I enjoy the memorization, but I persevered in order to please Andrew Swain, the local school teacher. I thought that if I could impress him adequately, perhaps he could help me in some way to go to a high school. Sambor, the local school, had no provision beyond the eighth grade.

A couple of years later, I attended a week of summer camp which the Canadian Sunday School Mission operated at Gimli, Manitoba. There the testimonies and the messages caused me to think seriously about my relation to the Lord. After a day or two, I became a believer in Christ as my Savior. The Scriptures I memorized played a vital part in my understanding of the Gospel.

Following that, I completed high school and a teacher training course in Winnipeg, and journeyed to Texas for more training. All through university and seminary, I kept asking individuals among faculty and students what plan they followed in memorizing Scripture. In most cases they had no specific plan.

All the time the Lord was moving me in a certain direction, though I was quite unaware of it. Locating in

Shreveport, Louisiana in 1943 as pastor of a small Cumberland Presbyterian mission church, I got a few people together, and in 1944 we announced in a full-page newspaper ad the Bible memorizing course which I had prepared. Nearly 600 enrolled. We had two weeks of camp, and that's how the work began.

Forty-nine years have now been expended in developing an effective Bible memorizing plan. The Spirit of God has surely guided and blessed in preparing the materials, including some forty-three memory books for all age levels. A large number of children, young people and adults throughout this land and in many parts of the world have been the recipients of God's manifold grace which invariably comes when His word is assimilated and appropriated. These blessings will continue to multiply with successive generations.

More than ever before, we are excited about memorizing the precious word of God. With ever-increasing zeal let us be faithful in telling others—both young and old—"You need to memorize Scripture."

There is a sense of deep gratitude to God for the saints, well known to Him, who are captives of this calling and who have prayed and who have invested much time and substance in this endeavor through the years. In the writing of this book, I am grateful for those who prayed, for those who graciously provided for the printing of it, and for those who helped in the writing and the proofreading. Together we pray that the urgent message of this book will be a blessing to all who read it, and that many will be motivated to memorize the Scriptures in this and in future generations. To God be all the honor and to God be all the glory!

St. Louis, Missouri　　　　　　N. A. Woychuk
March 1, 1993

1

Need

You do not need to memorize Scripture unless you clearly recognize the need.

You may not think much of memorizing God's word until you hear someone praying, and you notice how the word of God seems to fit in so powerfully as he prays. It is as if God was right there, speaking back. You are really lifted up by that prayer, and perhaps the thought drifts through your mind that you need to be memorizing some Scripture.

Your ability to express yourself may be very good, but you became aware of a serious lack in your witnessing when you heard a friend of yours dealing with a person and how he was able so neatly to convey the message convincingly by quoting just the right Scripture. That's when you say to yourself, perhaps, I need to be memorizing more Scripture.

But life goes on as usual until the storm hits. You lose your job. Your best friend moves out of town. On top of all that you become ill, and your very foundations are tested. You begin to be afraid, and you start searching for solid comfort and assurance. Perhaps it's then that you recall a verse you learned when you were just a child. You thought you had forgotten it, but here it is, just as clear as if you were reading it out of the Book: "What time I am afraid, I will trust in thee" (Ps. 56:3).

Without realizing fully what's involved, you recognize your great need and you say, I *must* memorize the word of God. He is the only One that can sustain me. I need the support of His word. I must know what God has to say to me every step of the way.

How can I walk and talk with God unless I have in mind some word of His to which I can respond, or which satisfies my questions and meets my need?

"This is where the rubber meets the road!"

Facing up to the existing need may not be the best motivation for memorizing Scripture, but it is a practical one and a good place to begin.

Maybe this is what prompted Mrs. Lien-Na Chai in Maryland to write the letter which I received this morning (June 6, 1991). She writes, "We are a Christian family. We would like to memorize Bible verses, but we don't know *how* to start. I have four children. My husband went to God's House in 1989. I would like to lead all my children to Christ."

We can tell from Mrs. Chai's letter that she recognizes her need. We believe that she and her family will indeed be memorizing Scripture with great profit and blessing. She knows that it is God's word that makes a person "wise unto salvation." "The entrance of Thy words giveth light; it giveth understanding unto the simple" (Ps. 119:130). As the children memorize the word of God, it will enable her to "lead" them to Christ.

Mrs. Chai probably knows also that Christians "grow" when they desire the sincere milk of the word and feed upon it (1 Pet. 2:2). When you have the strong desire for the word of God, you will not be satisfied with anything less.

We are completely dependent upon God not only for our physical food (Isa. 55:10), but even more so for our spiritual food which is provided for us in His word (Isa. 55:11). The word of God is "living" in the sense that it has the property of providing nutrition, and thereby sustaining life. It is a life-sustaining word. "The words that I speak unto you," our Lord said, "they are Spirit and they are life" (Jn. 6:63).

Physical food comes *up* "out of the earth" (Ps. 104:14) by divine arrangement, while spiritual food comes *down* to us from the heart of God in heaven.

Jeremiah said, "Thy words were found and I did eat them" (15:16). "Eat the good," Isaiah says, "and let your soul delight itself in abundance" (55:2).

The psalmist David was enraptured with the practical reality of the word. After describing its immeasurable power and value (Ps. 19:7-9), he exclaimed, "More to be desired are they than gold, yea, than much fine gold: sweeter also than honey and the honeycomb" (vs. 10).

And for those who assimilate it, internalize it and submit to it, "there is great reward" (vs. 11) — the reward of vision, the reward of power, the reward of manifold grace, the reward of enlargement of soul.

If you are going to memorize Scripture, approach it as heaven's greatest bounty for all people, for all generations.

Speaking of the incomparable potency of God's word about the time when the Bible was first being translated into the English language, *Edwin Sandys* (1519-1587) wrote, "This most precious jewel is to be preferred above all treasure:

"If thou be hungry, it is meat to satisfy thee;
if thou be thirsty, it is drink to refresh thee;
if thou be sick, it is a pleasant remedy;
if thou be weak, it is a staff to lean upon;
if thine enemy assault thee, it is a sword to fight with;
if thou be in darkness, it is a lantern
to illuminate thy path;
if thou be doubtful of the way,
it is a bright shining star to direct thee;
if thou be in displeasure with God,
it is the message of reconciliation;
if thou desire to save thy soul,
receive the engrafted word, for it is indeed
the word of life."

It is the consummate excellence and value of the Scriptures that makes us hunger for them.

How then shall I proceed to memorize God's word?

Where there is a sense of need and a growing desire to know God's word and to store it in mind and heart, there will surely come the ability to do it. Motivation is the important thing, not the techniques. Captivated by the practical value that the word will have for you in the varied situations of life, you will "eat" the words from heaven with great delight.

Perhaps the best way to "start" memorizing Scripture is to ask the Lord for divine help: "Lord, I believe Your word. I want to lay it up in my heart as You have commanded us to do. I want my children to memorize it so that they might personally come to know and trust the Lord Jesus as Savior. Help me, dear Lord, to find a plan of memorizing that will be profitable and which will encourage me to pursue it diligently day after day and year after year. I look to You for help and blessing. I pray in the name of Jesus Christ, our Lord. Amen."

2

Memory

"Memory," said Aeschylus, "is the mother of all wisdom," and "memory," Cicero agreed, "is the treasury and guardian of all things." The little girl, however, had a different view when she defined memory as "the thing I forget with."

God gave us memory, someone said, so that we might have roses in December.

Memory is our God-given power of retaining what we have learned, and recalling it at a later occasion. We fail to appreciate fully what a great trust God has given each one of us when, among many other endowments, He gave us the amazing capacities of the brain, including the one called memory.

Life would be virtually impossible without it. Memory underlies our ability to think rationally and to make decisions. All the movements in our daily life are determined by it. Imagine what it would be like if we tried to drive a car and did not remember which was the accelerator and which the brake pedal! In all situations, we react in accordance with what we remember. In the final analysis, we *know* only what we can accurately *remember*. Without the excellent faculty called memory, man would be a poor, destitute, naked being, making the same mistakes and falling into the same accidents again and again. All of life would be lived in the present moment.

In the practical aspects of life, we all seem to find it difficult to retain the things that excel. In part this may be due to the influence of the world system in which we live. We all struggle with the demands and tyranny of the immediate. Certain things in the course of making a living clamor for urgent attention. The failures of yesterday tend to oppress us; the uncertainty of the future makes us afraid.

Oliver Wendell Holmes said, "Memory is a crazy witch; she treasures bits of rags and straw, and throws her jewels out the window." Memory can be fickle and remain capricious even after we have become new creatures in Christ Jesus. We seem to forget how God has lifted us up out of the miry clay, and the way in which He has helped us all along life's journey. We forget His benefits. We forget,or take for granted, His mercy which endures forever.

Although "memory seems to have some very big holes through which some valuable things drop away into oblivion," as a dear saint remarked, yet it is only by the use of this faculty that we possess real knowledge and the riches of God's revelation.

The memory is like a secure bank. Money deposited in such a bank is not only safe, but it bears interest which accumulates with time. A memory stored with Scripture and enlightening "human" compositions is better than a large savings account. The precious promises of God will yield dividends, which though intangible, will be of more personal enrichment than material possessions.

Improving the Memory

Observation leads us to believe that there are some people who are endowed with prodigious memories at the time of birth. *Lord Macaulay* (1800-1859), who had an auricular mind, after hearing an oration, could repeat every word of it, as if he were reading it. Indeed he *was* reading it off the scroll of his brain which, like a sensitive photographic plate, recorded faithfully every sound it received. He could recite Milton's monumental epic, *Paradise Lost,* in its entirety. *Frances Ridley Havergal* (1836-1879) committed to memory all of the New Testament, the book of Psalms and Isaiah while still in her teens. Later she added all the Minor Prophets. Such people are the rare exceptions.

But we should not excuse ourselves from memorizing Scripture by saying that we have a "bad" memory. As a matter of fact, most of the authorities in this field staunchly maintain that there is no such thing as a "bad" memory. In time, the memory may gradually lose its reliability, not because it is bad, but due to inadequate exercise of it.

Our memories at any age level can be gradually improved by disciplined exercise and use of them. Do not be afraid to trust your memory. Test it. Put it to use. Do not allow it to grow weaker. We all know that any muscle or limb of the body is strengthened with proper exercise. *Milo,* the Greek athlete, sixth century B.C., six times victor in wrestling in both the Olympic and the Pythian games, took up a young calf and daily carried it on his shoulders. As the calf grew, his strength grew also, and he at last reached sufficient firmness of joints to bear the full-grown animal. Memorizing and reciting is to your mind what physical exercise is to the body.

Our memories will be gradually improved in

proportion to the exercise and use of them. If we do not try to use them, they will become almost lost. Those who are *inclined* to remember only a verse or two, will retain only a verse or two. Most folks, when asked to recite a Bible verse, will say John 3:16, and half of them will not recite it word-perfect. Those who have been accustomed to remember things but for an hour, will retain them but for an hour before they vanish.

Rise up, beloved, let the Spirit of God stir up your pure minds. Learn new Scripture. Charge your memories to retain. Repeat the verses a time or two and then attempt to recite them. Do not give up. Do not lose the priceless faculty of "remembering" as you grow older.

Instead of complaining that you have a "bad" memory, try to convince yourself that your memory is fine, but that it needs to be exercised. Do not give up. Begin the discipline that is required in memorizing.

Retaining and Recalling

Memorizing is generally characterized as a three-stage process: learning, retaining and recalling. Learning is the first stage in the memory process—trying to place the words and thought into your mind for the first time. This is called acquisition. There are two kinds of learning: that which is done intentionally and that which is done incidentally and unconsciously. You remember it without trying to remember it. You remember it because you have read it so many times with great delight.

Retaining is the storage of what has been learned. Your brain is likened to a large series of filing cabinets into which every single thing you see, hear and read is immediately filed. It is better retained if some attempt is made to categorize the material being learned.

Recalling or retrieving is the stage in which you try to bring back to mind the information that has been learned and retained. You will become aware that real memorization has occurred when you attempt to recall the verse you have learned.

Three Kinds of Memory

We may classify memorizing into three categories:

1) There is the *short-term memory*, lasting only a brief period of time. Every moment of our life, hundreds of impulses and impressions, stimulated by the senses, flow into the brain, and are for the most part promptly forgotten. They failed to arouse much interest; some of them are remembered only a few moments before they vanish.

2) The second category is the *medium-term memory*, which lasts a few hours and possibly extends into a day or two. This level of concentration enables a person to locate a certain house or remember a telephone number just long enough to dial it. This is probably the mediocre extent of concentration that is utilized in "cramming" for an exam. Most people engage in this type of memorization.

3) The highest level of concentration is the *long-term memory*, where certain impressions and information entering the brain register strongly. In the case of children, the *vividness* with which the information is presented helps to place it at once in the long-term memory. We purposefully store other information in our long-term memory because of its usefulness and importance. In this area of con-

centration, the person reacts with real enthusiasm and says to himself, consciously or unconsciously, I certainly want to remember this. He ponders on it purposefully. He commands his memory to retain it permanently. This is the approach we should always use in memorizing God's word.

Use It or Lose It

God has given you a memory: *use* it or *lose* it. Use it for the best possible purpose in laying up the precious word of the living God in your memory.

God has given you a healthy mind, a sound memory. God has given you His wonderful word. What is it that fills the spaces of your memory?

Supposing you had an expensive little chest, gold-plated and the lid studded with precious stones. Everybody marvels at it and is curious as to what such a rare encasement would contain. They are thoroughly intrigued and can hardly wait to see.

The lid is snapped open, and imagine their reaction when they notice the rubber bands, buttons, paper clips, old receipts, parking tickets, etc. What a disappointment! What a shame to have a valuable chest all lined in velvet, and to see it being used for collecting bits of trash.

That golden chest, friend, is your memory! God gave it to you so that you may store in it His precious word.

Delight in the blessed word of God! Allow it to excite your soul and captivate your whole attention. Think upon it, ponder it, enjoy it. Say with the psalmist, "O how love I Thy law; it is my meditation all the day" (119:97).

Test-time: Before you continue reading, say out loud two verses that you have memorized, possibly within the last year. Do you remember the references?

3
Why

In chapter one, we considered the "need" for memorizing the word of God.

Here, we will give attention to further basic reasons for treasuring up the Scriptures.

First, we must memorize Scripture because God commands us to do so.

God spoke to His people on Mount Sinai out of the midst of the fire, and the people responded by saying, "Behold, the Lord our God hath showed us His glory and His greatness, and we have heard His voice out of the midst of the fire: We have seen this day that God doth talk with man, and he liveth" (Deut. 5:24).

The people perceived that the great and glorious God expresses Himself in words that can be understood.

Immediately after that, God said, "And these words which I command thee this day, shall be in thine heart" (Deut. 6:6). God explained further that they were to put out the effort necessary to have His words in their hearts: "Therefore shall ye lay up these my words in your heart and in your soul" (Deut. 11:18).

God specifically commands us to memorize His

11

word so that we can have it in our hearts. This is His will and His plan for us. We cannot escape it. We dare not say to Him, "I don't have time," or "I just cannot memorize."

The second reason why we must memorize Scripture is because we cannot really "live" without it. In Deuteronomy chapter 8, we are told how God deals with His people, how He disciplines them, humbles them and lifts them up, that "He might make thee know that man doth not live by bread only, but by every word that proceedeth out of the mouth of the Lord doth man live" (Deut. 8:3).

We can exist all right without His word, but without it we cannot "live."

Why Memorize?

Since we have God's word printed nicely in a book which we may carry with us wherever we go, why is it necessary to go through all the effort of memorizing it?

As a matter of fact, I remember how a distinguished preacher once boasted before a large audience that he did not memorize Scripture. He inappropriately compared Scripture to the train schedule, and said with a self-assured satisfaction, "WHY should I memorize the train schedule when I have it in my pocket?" We will readily concede that he was wise in not memorizing the train schedule which is constantly subject to change. Furthermore, we are not told, "The train schedule have I hid in my heart that I might not sin . . ."

The travel schedule we may need five minutes or so a week, but the word of the living God is urgently needed 10,080 minutes a week, and having it in the mind and heart makes it instantly accessible at all times.

Yes indeed, daily *read* the word of God, daily *medi-*

tate on it, and your spirit will be daily exposed to the heart and mind of God.

Still much more profit is gained from *searching* and *studying* the Scriptures in some methodical way. *Martin Luther* compared Bible study to gathering apples. First shake the whole tree—read the whole Bible through just as you would read any other book. Then shake every limb, studying it book after book. Then shake every branch—give attention to every chapter. Then shake every twig by careful study of the paragraphs and sentences, and you will be greatly rewarded if you will then look under every leaf, by searching the meaning of each and every word.

In studying the word, we seek for truth not eloquence, we search after profit not subtle arguments, and best of all we yearn to find the Person of Christ on the sacred pages.

But the most effectual way of assimilating the word of God is by memorizing it, so that it is not a transient occurrence, like a caller who stays for an hour or so and continues on his journey; nay, this word of God is invited to remain in us, to settle down in us, to make its home in the inner soul and live in the deepest recesses of our being.

The Rationale

Why should I memorize *Scripture?*

Some years ago, the executive officer of a denomination with headquarters in Indiana wrote me to ask concerning some details regarding Scripture memorization. He stated that many of their people were suggesting memorizing the Scriptures, and then in what sounded like a distressing predicament, he said that his denomination had not even developed a *rationale* for Bible memorization. He proceeded to ask me if we had a rationale, and would I mind telling him

14

what it was, both from the Biblical, the educational, and the psychological points of view.

The letter was somewhat unusual, but basically it was sad. Here is a large group of presumably Christian people whose leading officer does not seem to know the value and the basic reasons for memorizing Scripture. Since then, however, I have come to believe that perhaps the serious lack of that denomination was not just an isolated case of the problem.

I prayed and considered the matter, and after a week or two I answered briefly as follows, "At the risk of being simplistic, I can say that we do indeed have a rationale for memorizing Scripture, and that it was established by God Himself many, many years ago. Here it is: (1) *'Thy word'*—that's the Biblical aspect of it. It is God's infallible, inerrant word that we are dealing with. (2) *'Have I hid in my heart'*—that's the educational or disciplinary part of it. It takes real effort to store up the word of God in the mind and heart, but it is exceedingly profitable. (3) *'That I might not sin against Thee'*—that's the psychological or spiritual aspect of it."

I concluded the letter by saying, " 'Thy word'— that's the best *possession*; 'have I hid in my heart'— that's the best *place*; 'that I might not sin against Thee'—that's the best *purpose*."

We memorize the Scriptures because they are the living words from God. We desire to have in our minds His words so that we may know at every turn what His will is for our lives.

One reason why many people do not take the word of God seriously is because they question the veracity of God, as Satan first did in Genesis 3:1: "Hath God said?"

The Bible is a miracle book! It came supernaturally through divine revelation (1 Cor. 2:10). God moved upon certain men called prophets and apostles in a special way, and made His will and His words known unto them. They wrote them down, "Not in words which man's wisdom teacheth, but which the Holy Spirit teacheth" (1 Cor. 2:13).

Paul denies the notion that they put down God's thoughts in their own words, or in words suggested by human learning. Peter confirms this fact when he said, "Holy men of God spake as they were moved by the Holy Ghost" (2 Pet. 1:21). The Bible came to us from God.

The Bible is superior to all other writings. Its excellence is infinitely superior, just as "the heavens are higher than the earth" (Isa. 55:9). The inspired writers themselves marvelled at its immeasureable greatness, "O Lord, how great are Thy works! and Thy thoughts are very deep" (Ps. 92:5). "Like a telescope, the Bible reaches beyond the stars and penetrates the heights of heaven and the depths of hell. Like a microscope, it discovers the minutest details of God's plan and purpose as well as the hidden secrets of the human heart" (L. S. Chafer).

Therefore, as the very word of God, it works effectually when it is personally received and appropriated as the word of God (1 Thess. 2:13). The famous surgeon, *Dr. Howard A. Kelly*, of Johns Hopkins fame, a staunch defender of the Bible as God's infallible word, described the practical reality of God's word thus, "The Bible appeals to me strongly as a physician, because it is such excellent medicine; it has never failed to cure a single patient if only he took his prescription honestly. It is in the spiritual therapeutics just what we so long for in all our bodily ailments, a universal remedy."

God's Word Is Indispensable

God wants us to realize that His word is not only

important but that it is absolutely *indispensable* in every sphere of life (Deut. 8:3).

God intends that the believer should live by the word daily and momentarily. His hidden life is to be sustained by it; his activities are to be guided by it. In every circumstance the quickening word of God will be his comfort and his consolation. Weighed down by sorrow, losses and disillusionment with friends, Job found his solace and sustenance in the word of God, of which he said, "I have esteemed the words of His mouth more than my necessary food" (23:12).

God's word is essential to keep us from failure (Josh. 1: 8). God's revelation is not just to be treated with high regard but it must be continually in our hearts and upon our lips all through the day and through the night seasons as well. The man whose "delight is in the law of the Lord," so that he "meditates" in it day and night, "shall be like a tree"—growing and flourishing—"and whatsoever he doeth shall prosper" (Ps. 1: 2-3). "Men," said *Calvin*, "never act skillfully, except insofar as they allow themselves to be ruled by the word of God."

God's word is essential to keep us from error (Matt. 22: 29). The Sadducees erred, Christ said, for two reasons: (1) They did not know the Scriptures. (2) They seriously underestimated the power of God. They argued and philosophized brilliantly about the problems of life in heaven but they were wrong because they did not perceive the meaning of the Old Testament Scriptures.

God's word is essential to keep us from sin (Ps. 119:11). The discovering word is to be treasured up in our hearts so as to become a source of power and life from within. Elsewhere the Psalmist said, "The law of his God is in his heart, none of his steps shall slide" (37: 31). Every day we have need of letting God's word probe the deepest recesses of our being to discover the hidden evil within, to search out every flaw and to restrain every tendency to do wrong. "By them is Thy servant warned, and in keeping of them there is great reward" (Ps. 19:11). God's word in the mind and heart continually is the most effective guard there is for our motives as well as our actions.

God's word is essential to keep us from stunted growth (1 Pet. 2:2). Where there is no heart longing for the divine milk, there is at once spiritual decline, which results in stunted spiritual growth. The word, like milk, is nourishing food, and it is delightful to the taste; by it we grow, and in it we taste the graciousness of God.

We live in a day when Bibles are accessible on every hand, but there is throughout the whole earth, as Amos prophesied, "a famine of hearing the words of the Lord" (8:11). Man does not seem to hear the blessed word of God addressing itself to the depths of his life; he pursues his own way, restless, wandering from sea to sea, craving some new thing, some new thrill, oblivious to the voice from Heaven. How exceedingly needful it is for man to accept the authority of God's law, and submit to the sovereign sway of the Holy Spirit in his life! This is the invitation and pleading of God in that dramatic call of the prophet Jeremiah, "O earth, earth, earth, hear the word of the Lord!" (22:29).

Dr. Dyson Hague (1857-1935), a Canadian, wrote an inspiring testimony: "The other day I took up the dear old Bible that my mother gave me, and I noted a verse in Genesis with a date written in the margin. There floated back upon my mind a time, some years ago, when I was in great trouble. I had to leave my dear wife, and children and to travel in quest of health in distant lands; my heart within me was sad, and one day opening the Bible at random, as they say, my eye caught these words in Genesis 28:15, 'Behold, I am with thee in all places whither thou goest, and will bring thee again into this land.'

"Shall I ever forget the flash of comfort that swept over my soul as I read that verse! All the exegetes and critics in the world could never persuade my soul that it was a far-off echo of a Babylonian legend, or some relic of an Oriental myth. No, no. That was a message to me. It swept into my soul as a voice from heaven. It lifted me up, and no man will ever shake me out of the conviction that that message that day was God's own word to me, inspiring because inspired, inspired because inspiring."

Though written a long time ago, God's word is just as personal and just as appropriate as if it came this very day to give each believer the needed endurance, comfort and hope (Rom. 15:4). It flames in the believer's heart with a celestial light; it quickens faith, purifies purpose and strengthens the will. Generation succeeds generation, but each finds the Bible fresh. It does not become obsolete. This is a fact of immense significance; and its only explanation is that the Bible is a *living* book, the word of the *living* God. All other books partake of the infirmity of their authors, and are either dying or dead.

The great literary scholar and educator of the nineteenth century, *Matthew Arnold*, said, "To the Bible men will return because they cannot do without it; because happiness belongs to righteousness, and righteousness is revealed in the Bible. For this simple reason men will return to the Bible, just as a man who tried to give up food, thinking that it was a vain thing and that he could do without it, would return to food."

Each generation in turn surveys the pledged word of God, and then says, "There hath not failed one word of all His good promise" (1 Kings 8:56; Josh. 21:45).

4

Interest

Memorizing depends upon interest. You hear or read something significant and you say to yourself, "that really interests me. I like it. I want to remember it." You at once proceed to write it down, keep it before you and think upon it.

Becoming vitally interested in the word of God usually comes as a result of contact with that special person whom God brings into your life. You see what it is doing for him or her. You are impressed and you want to have the word in *your* mind. You noticed how he was "addicted" to God's word. You talked with him and somehow you begin to think like he does. You see, real interest in the word of God is a contagion. It is *caught* more than it is *taught*.

Now, are you interested in memorizing Scripture? Have you "caught" the enthusiasm?

You surely must be interested in memorizing Scripture or you would not be reading this book.

Memorizing Scripture begins with a keen interest in wanting to remember it because you believe it will be of real value to you in meeting the needs in your life.

Memorizing is generally not a question of *ability*

but of *interest* and desire. If you are truly interested and desire to do it, then you have already "stepped on the starter," and the engine of your brain is already running. Motive in memorizing is basic. Intention predisposes the memory for retention. Motive is that which induces you to act. You are interested, and you seize upon a particular portion of Scripture and purpose to spend time and mental resources in assimilating it. Your persistence in memorizing it will depend almost entirely upon the *extent* of your interest.

Keep that particular Scripture that interests you constantly before you, and begin repeating it. Say it out loud and engage your hearing apparatus in functioning for you. As you dwell on the thought and truth of God's word, enjoy it and allow it to lift your soul and spirit heavenward.

David was not only interested in the word, he *delighted* in it. He said, "I will delight myself in Thy statutes" (Ps. 119:16). I will enjoy them, relish them and feast upon them. Then he said, "I will not forget Thy word." Because I find such delight in Thy word, I purpose to memorize it. I want to remember it. I will not forget it. I will lay it up in my mind where I can meditate on it day and night, and receive the blessing and the strength that God purposed for me to have.

The psalmist regarded God's word as being of more value to him than "gold." Money can never buy the value and satisfaction derived from it. It is "sweeter than honey" (Ps. 19:10), and the lingering taste of it makes us long for more of it.

David's vital interest in the word of the Lord is further expressed throughout that word-filled Psalm 119: "I will never forget Thy precepts: for with them Thou hast quickened me" (93). "O how love I Thy law! it is my meditation all the day" (97). "Thy testimonies have I taken as an heritage forever; for they are the rejoicing of my heart" (111). "Thy testimonies are wonderful: therefore doth my soul keep them" (129). "Thy word is very pure; therefore Thy servant loveth it" (140). "Concerning Thy testimonies, I have known of old that Thou hast founded them for ever" (152). "I rejoice at Thy word, as one that findeth great spoil" (162).

Put it down, friend, and always remember that memorizing Scripture depends on your interest. Delighting in that Scripture will sustain your interest and keep you going. "Eat the good" the prophet Isaiah said, "and let your soul delight itself in abundance" (55:2). Let your inner man have a spiritual feast.

The Bible is a wonderful book, but as *General Gordon* used to say, "After all, the chief proof that the Bible is good food is the eating of it." Exactly so! Chemical investigation into the ingredients of a loaf of bread has its needful place, no doubt, but the analyst's household would starve, if they hesitate to feed upon it until the analysis has been completed to his entire satisfaction.

Reading and studying God's word gets the person into the word, but memorizing it gets the word into the person, and there it becomes a major force in molding the spiritual life and conforming it to the will of God.

Do not waste any time fretting about the notion that you may not remember it. Keep at it. Do not idle away your time any more. Sloth, indolence and idleness will no more bless the mind with spiritual riches, than it will fill the hand with grain, the field with corn, and the purse with treasure.

In pursuing the memorization of Scripture, we must diligently resist the influences of the world around us. "The ear must be turned away from the sounds of earthly pleasures, the din of worldliness, the voice of human speculation, and must listen attentively to communications from the spiritual and eternal" (*D. Thomas*).

Oh that we might truly hunger for the blessed word of God, and constantly be renewed in our minds so that we will not allow the world's philosophies to squeeze us into their mold.

"There is a real danger," wrote *Fred Schuppe, Virginia,* some years ago, "of being shaped or conformed to the world by all the forces and pressures at work, such as the radio, television, current magazines, newspapers, what the stream of society thinks, and the like. Practically everything we see, hear or read is contrary to the philosophy and thinking of the word of God.

"The foregoing is negative. The positive is to be *transformed* by the renewing of our minds. I need to have my mind renewed, restored, constantly brought back to its original moorings by the word of God and by the Spirit of God. What does *He* say? What is *His* will? What are *His* purposes for me? God forbid that my thinking, my philosophy of life, my purposes for living should be molded by Wall Street, by Hollywood, by Madison Avenue or by Paris stylists."

Meditating and delighting in the precious word of the living God is what enables the believer not to be adversely influenced by the unbelievers or by the carnal Christians around us. The believer, young or older, who has the word in his heart and on his tongue tip will not "walk in the counsel of the ungodly, nor stand in the way of sinners, nor sit in the seat of the scornful" (Ps. 1:1). Such a person is indeed "blessed."

As you enjoy memorizing the Scriptures, there will soon awaken in you a strong desire to see others around you—at home, at work, at school, and at your church—taking hold of the word and laying it up in their hearts. This morning (July 8, 1991), I read a letter from a *Mrs. A. B. Creecy, Jr.* in west Texas where she says, "I am interested in involving our whole church in Scripture Memory as my husband and myself were personally involved in your program several years ago. Send me whatever materials I need in order to enroll people of all ages."

That is indeed a noble aspiration!

Dr. J. R. Miller, whose devotional books written several decades ago, I highly prize, said, "The *very best thing* we can do for people in this world of sin and sorrow is to get the words of Christ into their hearts. The living Christ walks among the glades of God's word, and we meet Him there in sweet communion as we meditate therein day and night!"

But Mrs. Creecy and her husband face a big task. People in our churches do not appear interested. It seems that it is at least six times more difficult today to arouse people even in an evangelical Bible church to memorize Scripture than it was thirty years ago. They prefer to sit in the pew and listen effortlessly to the able preacher. They may look spiritual and appear wise but have nothing of the word of God in their minds, and have no special interest in undertaking the disciplining effort of memorizing it.

But we will not give up. We will pray for them. We will pursue them. We will talk to their children. We will persist with it, and although we may not succeed in getting the whole church involved, we will surely succeed by the grace of God to stir up that needed *interest* in the lives of some. God commands us to memorize His word, and we cannot "live" without it.

Spirit of the living God, evermore, create that interest and hunger for the word in the lives of Thy people!

5

Plan

Now that you are interested and have a real desire to memorize the Word of God, the next important matter is the *plan*. What portion of the Scriptures will you undertake to memorize? This is a very important step, because sometimes disappointment in a certain plan may turn a person off from memorizing Scripture.

Remember, however, that no plan will automatically assure you that you will succeed in storing up God's word. You must put out the mental energy no matter what plan you follow.

It is a universal fact, that unless we have a workable plan, including a specific recitation schedule, we will not get very far with memorizing Scripture, irrespective of how highly we may value it or how urgently we may desire to do it. During ten years of university and seminary, I asked a large number of students and faculty what "plan" they followed in committing Scripture to memory. Probably more than ninety percent had no plan. But we seldom accomplish anything worthwhile in any field of endeavor without a definite plan. This is true in business. This is true in school and at home. It is certainly true in our spiritual progress.

(1) One plan that some people follow is that of memorizing certain verses in connection with daily Bible reading and quiet time. Significant verses are checked or underlined and an effort is made to memorize them. This seems to work for some people very well, but it may lack sufficient organizational structure to be followed for a long time.

(2) Memorizing certain chapters or an entire Book in the Bible is often undertaken. When implemented with systematic effort, such a plan has some obvious advantages in that you follow the sequence of thought and learn the verses in their context. There is difficulty sometimes in trying to lay hold of the exact verse in the chapter that you desire.

John Ruskin's mother selected certain chapters that he was required to memorize; among them was the 119th Psalm. She succeeded in making him memorize it; and not only that, it had to be done word-perfect and recited with expression so as to indicate that he really understood what he had memorized.

David Pent thrills people at some of the conventions by proving to them that he knows the entire New Testament from memory. *Frances Ridley Havergal*, as I have mentioned before, memorized the entire New Testament and several Old Testament Books. There are many others who have excelled in memorizing the word of God in this manner.

(3) Typing or printing the desired Bible verses on small cards has been used quite successfully in memorizing the word. The Scripture text is printed generally on one side and the reference on the other. Many individuals have developed such a system for themselves, but it has been best perfected by the *Navigators* and the *Young Life Campaign,* who have arranged the verses under topical headings and assembled them in

packs for handy use. The plan has certain merits and many have been blessed in following it. More recently another plan has outline pictures on the cards. These are to form a clue for remembering the verse.

(4) The Scripture Memory Fellowship has Bible verses printed in attractive and handy memory books for all age levels. Each book bears a title which represents the subject covered in the book, and the verses in the book are arranged in poetry-like style and set under instructive topics or themes. The Scriptures organized under headings enables a person to associate them with the particular topic and to be helped in recalling them more readily.

A newcomer to the pharmacy will learn the names of the medicines in the shop much sooner when they are properly labelled and arranged on the shelves in an orderly manner. People following the Scripture Memory system do not memorize scattered verses but verses which form a connection under the meaningful assignment topics.

Although there are certain advantages in learning the Scripture by chapters or by books as stated above, the fact is that in our everyday life we seldom use them that way. We do not normally recall large portions of the Bible in the practical situations that arise. This is true in the experience of children as well as adults. We generally lay hold of just a verse or two, whether it be in that moment of need or in that unexpected opportunity for witness. The main purpose of memorizing Scripture is certainly not just for the sake of knowledge but in order that we might be better equipped to draw on these Scriptures in our real life situations.

A good example of this is how the Lord Himself used the Scriptures. Having been without food for forty days, He was challenged by Satan to change a stone into bread and satisfy His hunger. Christ did not respond by reciting the entire Book of Deuteronomy, nor did He even quote a chapter. He simply seized upon part of Deuteronomy 8:3 and said, "It is written, man shall not live by bread alone, but by every word that proceedeth out of the mouth of God" (Matt. 4:4).

When Satan, who apparently knows Scripture and knows its power perhaps better than we do (Luke 8: 12), resorted to using it, our Lord simply recalled another Scripture and said, "It is written again . . ." By His skillful use of the sword of the Spirit, He soon cut Satan down. In reading the Book of Acts, it is amazing to see how much of God's word the Lord's disciples had stored up and how they used it after the example of the Lord Jesus Christ.

The Underlying Philosophy

This is the underlying philosophy in the organization and writing of the forty-three Bible memory books which the Lord has enabled me to develop for all age levels. This concept guided me in the careful preparation of the assignment headings and the selection of the most appropriate Scriptures in each book and under each particular heading. The vital principle always kept in mind was how best to help the child, the young person or the adult in his daily use of God's word.

An appropriate word from *Dr. Justin Long*, Maryland: "I have greatly appreciated learning verses in the systematic manner because of the way the verses are organized by topics; this arrangement not only makes memorizing easier for me but helps explain the significance of the verses."

The structured memory work in the Scripture Memory system is available for all age levels beginning with the preschool children, the grade school, the intermediate, the high school, the college ages and also the adults.

We know that our plan of memorizing the word works effectively and has helped over a million people to do it, but we want to make it clear that our system does not guarantee results unless you use it properly and give it the time and effort required. Our plan does not aim at helping you become "mental wizards" where you can learn Scriptures without much effort. This system represents a way of life where the whole family is engaged in memorizing the word, and this continues year after year. Some families have continued in it for twenty, thirty and forty years successively. You may have tried a plan—where you lurch forward —and then sputter and stop.

A good system of Bible memorizing will not overlook the establishment of rules for learning the verses and a prescribed schedule for the recitation of each assignment. These requirements of learning and reciting must be diligently maintained, or else procrastination and excuses will cause the entire effort to fail.

A good plan of committing the eternal word to memory must be regarded like a school. It is taken seriously. The learning goes on day by day, and the students submit to the required tests at the stated times. This makes for a disciplinary type of learning and brings about wonderful results. Participants in our system spend time throughout the week in learning the given number of verses in each assignment and are required to recite the assignment at a stated time.

Deciding on the best segment of weeks for the memorizing course and the arranging of a definite recitation schedule must be developed with studied attention to all details. When the recitation schedule has been determined, it should be reproduced and presented to each memorizer. The importance of adhering to the recitation schedule cannot be overestimated.

Requirements

There must be accountability.

Mrs. Shirley Shackelford, Texas, who became a believer through memorizing the word in our system, writes, "Scripture Memory Fellowship gives our family the structure and incentive to accomplish Scripture memorization. We believe memorization is important, but until we have specific verses assigned to be recited on a certain date, we just never seem to 'get around to it.' We need the *accountability* it requires of us and the rewards are fun to anticipate, especially for the children.

"We are in the second year of homeschooling our fifteen year old daughter, but this is her tenth year in Scripture Memory. This ministry has been the most important organization, except for her family, in encouraging her in 'growing in grace and the knowledge of our Lord and Savior, Jesus Christ.' "

The person who undertakes to be the hearer or supervisor assumes a big responsibility for the success of the program. In our system a Supervisor Guide is provided. Memorizers must be willing to submit to the leadership and direction of the supervisor.

Memorizers at work often recite to another person during lunch break. Imagine reciting the verses to the unsaved! Although they may suspect that you have sought the arrangement for their benefit, yet they can hardly take exception because you are definitely engaged in a system which calls for a hearer.

The blessing of memorizing Scripture in a systematic way has been most gratifying and far-reaching. *Mrs. Frank Toman* in Ontario, Canada, readily attests to this: "Personally, I find your way of memorizing just what I need for both Bible knowledge, meditation and instruction. As a family, we have been memorizing for twelve years. It sure helps when Mom or Dad (or both) are in it, too. The children realize that we feel it is important. This gives us as parents an informal opportunity to discuss spiritual truths with the children personally."

Another comprehensive testimony comes from a Tennessee business man, *Mr. Harold R. Stephens*: "I never cease to marvel at the tremendous way that God is using this systematic method of Scripture memorization to enlighten darkened minds to their need of the Savior, and to afford the believer a better understanding of all the unlimited resources with which he is provided, as a member of the Body of Christ.

"I can truthfully say, that as a result of my participation in this wonderful program of hiding God's Word away in my heart, I have a better understanding, and a greater love for the inspired Word of God, than could have been derived from any other method I might have followed.

"I will forever be grateful to God for having provided such an effective program and the human instrument for the initiation of this wonderful program, and for its perpetuation for these many years."

6

Incentives

The use of incentives is a major factor in motivating children and young people in applying themselves diligently to the task of memorizing Scripture. It's amazing how even adults respond to the idea of receiving rewards.

Charles H. Spurgeon, of London and world fame, tells how his grandmother *paid* him to memorize Scripture and Isaac Watts hymns.

She promised to pay him a penny for each Scripture or hymn that he could recite perfectly. He learned them so rapidly that she found it necessary first to reduce the reward to a halfpenny and later to a farthing. "There is no telling," Spurgeon said, "how low the amount might have sunk, but grandfather came to her rescue. Since he was getting overrun with rats in his warehouse, he offered me a shilling a dozen for all I could kill."

Spurgeon later recalled that the occupation of rat-killing paid better and was much more fun, but that learning the Scriptures and hymns were permanently profitable and were assets which undergirded all his ministry.

The wise and godly grandmother offered money for getting her grandson to assimilate spiritual truth, and he responded enthusiastically. Incentives play an important role in providing motivation and perseverance.

Do Rewards Corrupt Motives?

There are a few people here and there who object to the idea of rewards for memorizing Scripture. I recall years ago, a distinguished leader who denounced it as being "immoral," and he did so in the city where we were headquartered.

There was also a leader in a prominent church in Boston who strenuously objected to it, and said that our youth should be trained to memorize God's holy word for the love of it and not because of some prizes. He claimed that the reward system tended to corrupt their motives.

I inquired of some of his members at the time if they paid their pastor a salary, and they said they did. Now then, I asked, might not compensating their pastor for preaching corrupt his motives? Should not he be willing to preach for the love of preaching and because of the eternal reward that would be his as a result?

No, no, it's not "immoral" to offer rewards for memorizing Scripture, and it will not "corrupt motives." Let's be realistic in all this. All of life is based on the incentive principle. You go to work regularly, day after day. Of course, you love your work and feel you are making a contribution to the well-being of others, but, basically, is it not the paycheck that sustains your diligent workmanship?

Let's face it. Children and young people generally do not recognize the value of Scripture even on a par with other subjects they study in school. They consent to the idea that the word is good for them, and they may do this to a great extent because they have heard this emphasis from parents, pastor and teachers whose judgment they normally respect. But their own evaluation of the word is not that keen.

Literally hundreds of people across this nation have told me that when they first enrolled in our system, they did so strictly to get the rewards. Some stated that it was the prospect of the week at camp that kept them going. But is it not wonderful how the Lord turns it around, and the memorizer soon discovers with delight, as the years advance, that the greatest reward is having the Scripture abiding in his heart?

> *Father of mercies, in Thy Word*
> *What endless glory shines!*
> *For ever by Thy name adored*
> *For these celestial lines.*
>
> *O may these heavenly pages be*
> *'My ever dear delight;*
> *And still new beauties may I see,*
> *And still increasing light.*
>
> *Divine Instructor, gracious Lord,*
> *Be Thou for ever near;*
> *Teach me to love Thy sacred Word,*
> *And view my Saviour there.*
>
> *—A. Steele*

Therefore, let us not be disturbed in the least if the reward seems to be the person's primary goal instead of the Scripture he is asked to memorize.

Example of Daniel Webster:

Daniel Webster (1752-1852), the silver-tongued orator and one of America's greatest statesmen, was grounded in the Scriptures in his early years.

Professor James Tappan came to Salisbury, New Hampshire, for an eight week teaching session.

"We're going to have a contest during this term," he announced on the first day of school to the eleven girls and five boys who were present.

"For the boy who memorizes the most verses from the Holy Scriptures during the next eight weeks," he said, as he dramatically held a brand-new shiny jack-knife overhead, "This will be the prize."

Daniel spent fewer days looking for chestnuts in the woods with other boys. He already knew quite a number of Bible verses by heart. Now was his chance to have a knife all his own. Money was scarce in the Webster household, and there was no way he could earn enough money. So he just *had to win* that knife Mr. Tappan offered, even though he was one of the youngest boys in school.

As soon as he got home, he got the Bible and put it on the kitchen table. His sister Abigail was right by his side. "Are you going to try to win that lace Mr. Tappan offered the girls?" he asked. "If you are, we can help each other learn the verses."

Abigail said "yes," and the two worked faithfully on their verses day after day and week after week.

On the day the contest ended, Professor Tappan had each student come to the front of the room to recite. Someone quoted twenty-five verses. Then another quoted forty, and another quoted fifty-two Bible verses. Then it was Daniel's turn.

Walking confidently to the front of the little one-room school, he turned to face Mr. Tappan and his classmates.

"I will begin with Psalm 1." The schoolmaster marked them off on the blackboard under Daniel's name. Then he recited twelve verses in Psalm 2, eight in Psalm 3, eight in Psalm 4, twelve in Psalm 5, ten in Psalm 6. Daniel was now in the lead, but he kept going until he had recited one hundred and twenty verses with never a pause and never a single mistake.

"Enough," called the schoolmaster, as Daniel drew a quick breath in preparation to recite more.

"I declare Daniel Webster the winner of the jack-knife."

Frequently, motivation can be achieved in other ways. *Marylyn Beasley, Tennessee,* was only eight years old, but she was able to memorize and recite what her High School sisters were doing, and being able to keep up with her older sisters motivated her.

A word of commendation from a parent or some respected Christian leader exerts a powerful influence. Being asked to recite Scripture at a service is a means of real encouragement. Planned recognition of those who engage in systematic memorization inspires many a youth to press on with patience and perseverance.

While still in grade school at Sky Lake, Manitoba, 80 miles north of Winnipeg, I memorized 500 Bible verses and recited them to Mr. Andrew Swain, the teacher at Sambor school. I did not understand the Bible verses nor can I say that I enjoyed them, but I did it in order to ingratiate myself with the teacher. Although a reward of a week at camp was promised, my main objective was to impress Mr. Swain with my ability to learn in the hope that he might be able in some way to assist me in going to high school, since Sambor provided no schooling beyond the eighth grade.

Sometimes parents would do almost anything to get their children to memorize Scripture. I remember back in the sixties when the father of an affluent family in Texas asked me what I thought about the idea he had of offering his teen age son a new car if the boy would memorize Book 1 in the High School series. He was very concerned about the boy's spiritual welfare. I was rather surprised at so lavish an offer, but I admired his concern, and encouraged him to go ahead. I'm not sure I was ever told what happened in that case.

One cannot help but wonder what incentives Mr. & Mrs. Jesse used with their youngest son, David, in encouraging him to memorize Scripture! Maybe they offered him a special camping trip at Elim (Ex. 15: 27), or perhaps they promised him a brand new harp when he completed the "Moses Series" of Bible memorization. But we have only to read some of his Psalms, like 19 and 119, and see how he delighted in the Scriptures.

Scripture Memory System of Rewards:

After seeking to challenge people—young and older—for many years to memorize God's word, I am convinced that a good incentive system is almost indispensable in obtaining good results in memorizing the word of God. This is true in working with an individual, with a whole group in a church or community, and it is true to a great extent also in the Christian school. Furthermore, we have learned that the most effective incentives are those which exert a strong spiritual influence and augment the blessing of the word itself.

In the work of Scripture Memory Fellowship, we offer every memorizer, as of the present time, four rewards. The rewards are carefully selected in order to contribute to the spiritual progress of the memorizer. Through the years, many families have built libraries of good Christian books which they count among their most valued possessions. Often these are books which they would never have acquired in any other way. We offer Christian fiction books for lighter reading, Bible stories for children, puzzle books, biographies, devotional books, Bible commentaries and reference works. We have also developed Bible games which draw the family together and provide hours of enjoyment while getting acquainted with Scriptural concepts and facts. Plaques, posters, cassettes and song books are also offered. We also prepare Review-Achievement Folders for all the memorizers and an attractive personalized lasered-wood plaque for those who complete the five memory books in any series.

We strive for books that are attractive, practical and instructive for the different age levels.

The offer of a substantial part of the cost of a week at an SMF camp has tremendous appeal to the older children and young people. *Pamela Braithwaite's* new book, "Byron's Double Discovery" points out effectively the value of a week at camp as well as the blessings of memorizing Scripture in a carefully prepared plan.

Care must always be taken to make sure that we give what we promise. The rewards should be given promptly and as scheduled. They should be presented in a manner so as to make the most of the occasion, not only in commending the memorizers but also in arousing the interest of those who are observing.

This kind of a reward system is not easy to achieve, especially when the enrollment fee is nominal and in no way covers the entire cost involved. Those who may be hard pressed financially are encouraged to enroll without paying the enrollment fee or by paying it later. We depend heavily upon the prayers and interest of the Lord's people in this ministry.

Long Range Results:

What about the long range outcome of all this?

Charles Haddon Spurgeon memorized the Scriptures and hymns in order to collect the "farthings" from his dear grandmother, but those eternal words abounded richly in his mind and heart and made his sermons truly "Bibline," and he being dead, "yet speaketh" through those sermons which continue to be reprinted.

The verses I memorized to please the school teacher were of no value to me at the time I did it, but a couple of years later, I stayed awake all night recalling those verses I had memorized. God used them in a wonderful way that week at camp in making me "wise unto salvation."

Daniel Webster memorized the Scriptures to capture that shiny knife which later he sold to his brother Zeke for fifteen cents, but he put the things he learned to good use even as a young lad. As he watered the horses of the teamsters who stopped at his father's tavern, he surprised the men by reciting the Scriptures and the hymns to them. The Scriptural principles which he learned early in life molded his thinking and gave depth and perception to him all throughout his distinguished career as one of America's three greatest statesmen, who developed the solid foundations for the greatest nation on the face of the earth.

In his memorial address in Boston, on October 28, 1852, *Rufus Choate* made pointed reference to Webster's "giant infancy" in that his training included "catechism and Bible and Watts' version of the Psalms."

In 1823, Daniel Webster, not a preacher but a statesman who was grounded in the truth of the Bible, said, "If religious books are not widely circulated among the masses in this country, I do not know what is going to happen to us as a nation. If truth be not diffused, error will be; if God and His Word are not known and received, the devil and his works will gain the ascendancy; if the evangelical volume does not reach every hamlet, the pages of corrupt and licentious literature will; if the power of the Gospel is not felt throughout the length and breadth of the land, anarchy and misrule, degradation and misery, corruption and darkness, will reign without mitigation or end."

Those meaningful words are just as appropriate for our times as if they were spoken today.

Yes, encourage our youth to memorize God's word by providing substantial incentives, preferably the kind which will add to their spiritual stature. Soon they will discover for themselves that God's word stored in mind and heart is their abiding reward. They will find out that it is "sweeter than honey" and "more to be desired than gold" (Ps. 19:10).

Hopefully they will never stop memorizing and meditating on the Scriptures.

"My son," God says through Solomon, "keep thy father's commandment, and forsake not the law of thy mother" (Prov. 6:20). In the context we learn that the father's "commandment" and the mother's "law" refer to the "lamp" and "light" of God's word.

The next verse tells what a young person must do with God's word: "Bind them continually upon thine heart, and tie them about thy neck." *Delitzsch* suggests that the word "bind" is equivalent to the Latin, "circumplicare," which means to wind round and round about an object. Just as the little "bouncer" in a golf ball is made more substantial and resilient with the winding of the many rounds of rubberized cord, so the word of God increases the strength and agility of the person who assimilates the Scriptures "continually."

The word of the living God is to be always present and always affecting the whole of a person's life. The "heart" suggests that the Scriptures shall be vitally controlling the affections and decisions, and the "neck" suggests that the Scriptures will be an ornament adorning the moral character. The results are most gratifying.

Here is what happens in the life of the person who is *continually* nourished with the word of life (Prov. 6: 22):

(1) *"When thou goest, it shall lead thee"*—The word treasured up in the heart shall be a sure guide. "And thine ears shall hear a word behind thee, saying, "This is the way, walk ye in it . . ." (Isa. 30:21).

(2) *"When thou sleepest, it shall keep thee"*—The word in mind and heart will be your ever-present keeper throughout the night seasons, when His "speech shall distil as the dew" (Deut. 32:2) and afford you that perfect peace and security. "I will both lay me down in peace, and sleep: for Thou Lord, only makest me dwell in safety" (Ps. 4:8).

(3) *"When thou awakest, it shall talk with thee"*— When you arise in the morning, this word which you are "continually" binding round your heart, will converse and commune with you. It will immediately make you aware of the Lord's nearness and companionship.

> *Oh, how I love this word, this wonder book*
> *That God has given men! So rich, so sweet,*
> *So full of truth and light, of drink and meat*
> *And priceless treasures for eyes which look*
> *With faith and prayer upon its script! O brook*
> *No task to crowd it out, but pause to greet*
> *The Master here each day in soul retreat.*
>
> —Gwynn M. Day

7

Examples

Possessing the property of the word internally is great gain.

Internalizing the word of God so as to involve the whole being—mind, soul and spirit—is the means of spiritual prosperity and fruitfulness.

A little later in this chapter we will examine some examples of getting others to *internalize* Scripture.

Knowing some Bible stories, historical facts, Bible names and a general knowledge of the Bible is not the same as having portions of the exact words of God in your memory. Christians generally fail to see this distinction. It is good to know the books of the Bible and be able to relate some of the Bible stories, but this is not the same as being able to recall the exact words given us from God.

For example, it is always interesting to remember a few things about Psalm 23, but it is so exceedingly profitable to be able to recall that Psalm word-for-word—"The Lord is my shepherd." Therefore, "I shall not want."

Every word of God is pure! Every word of God is perfect! Every word of God is powerful! The Holy

Spirit resides in those words. Those words give rise to faith; this enables us to walk by faith.

We must lay hold of the very words of God. We must internalize the distinctive property of the Scriptures. We must treasure them. We must believe them. We must think upon them. We must meditate upon them day and night. They are the means of our spiritual existence.

At the homeschooling conventions, I try to show the difference between knowing some things about the word and having the property of the word in memory, and usually the attentive listeners stand amazed.

Eating the Word

In that remarkable 55th chapter, God asks some practical questions through the prophet Isaiah, "Wherefore do you spend money for that which is not bread? and your labor for that which satisfieth not?" Why do you spend hard-earned money and exhausting labor for that which does not bring lasting satisfaction?

Then, God points emphatically to something that is superior, "Hearken diligently unto Me," He says, "and eat ye that which is good, and let your soul delight itself in fatness" (Isa. 55:2).

You will notice in your Bible that in the sentence "eat *ye that which is* good" the words in italics are not in the original, but are supplied for smoother reading. Literally, it says, "Eat the good." Eat that which is really nourishing and satisfying. From the context of the chapter, there is little doubt but that "the good" refers to the word of God. "Eat the good, and let your soul delight itself in abundance."

Do not just admire the word of God! Eat it! Assimilate it. Seize upon it with relish. Do not just nibble on it! Eat big mouth-fuls—devour it.

"It is blessed to eat into the very soul of the Bible," said C. H. Spurgeon, "until at last you come to talk in Scriptural language, and your spirit is flavored with the words of the Lord, so that your blood is Bibline and the very essence of the Bible flows from you."

Internalizing the word of God is what this ministry is all about.

Eating the word of God is like holding the food in your mouth and getting the full taste of it. Turn it round and round, thinking of it from this point of view and from that, talking about it, and in the whole process sinking it into the chambers of your memory and assimilating it into the bloodstream of your spiritual life.

Implanting the Property of the Word

Learning things about the Bible is good, but the chief responsibility of the parent or the teacher is that of implanting or installing the property of the word itself in the mind and heart of the student. This does not happen by chance or by some hit-or-miss effort. It is accomplished by design—by the use of a plan that is carefully developed.

At this point I am going to lead the parent and the teacher through an actual process of accomplishing this.

Are you ready? I will pose a couple of examples.

Here is Monica Augustine in Rome, Georgia. She is homeschooling Josiah (Jo for short), her eleven-year-old son.

She is undertaking to help him memorize Bible verses in the Scripture Memory Book 5 titled, "Pleasing God," where six carefully selected Bible verses will be memorized in the course of one week.

The title of the first assignment is "Pleasing God in My Thought."

He learns the title of the Book and the title of each assignment as he moves along.

First Day

Right after breakfast, Monica regularly set aside a half hour or so for "eating the word." The first verse is Job 42:2, "I know that Thou canst do everything, and that no thought can be withholden from Thee."

The mother explained the meaning of the verse.

Monica had Jo read it over two or three times. Then she had Jo try to recite the assignment heading and the verse: "Assignment 1 - Pleasing God in My Thought - I know that Thou canst do everything, and that no thought can be withholden from Thee, Job 42: 2."

When Jo hesitated on some of it, she gently prompted him with a word or an idea suggested by the word. Then she had him recite it all again two or three times.

Then Monica led in a simple prayer asking God to help Jo retain the verse in his mind.

Following lunch, they came back to Job 42:2. Jo was asked to recite the assignment heading, the verse and the reference. Only this time she insisted that her son give the recitation with good expression in order to make sure that he understood what he was reciting. She asked Jo questions about the meaning of the verse. She filled in explanations as it appeared necessary.

Monica encouraged Jo to think about that verse throughout the afternoon as much as possible.

As the family sat down together for dinner, Monica asked Jo to recite the verse before the prayer of thanks for the food was offered. As a matter of fact, the whole family began to recite the verse together. As the meal progressed, Monica asked Jo if he thought of the verse throughout the afternoon, and if he were able to apply it in some situation. The whole family joined in the conversation about it.

At bed time, Jo recited the verse again with much more enjoyment. The father led in prayer, and Jo dozed off into sleep with the words of God upon his mind.

Second Day

Monica followed the same procedure with the second verse, which is Psalm 19:14:

> "Let the words of my mouth,
>   and the meditation of my heart,
>   be acceptable in Thy sight, O Lord,
>   my strength and my Redeemer."

In reciting the second verse, Monica required that Jo recite again the assignment heading and the first verse he learned before attempting to recite the next verse.

Monica did this for six days in a row, and the whole family was excited when Jo stood up and recited the title of the book, the assignment heading, the verses and the references—six Bible verses were now implanted in the mind of this fifth-grade scholar.

When Jeremiah (Jerry for short) learned that his friend Jo was memorizing Scripture, he was overjoyed. He commended his friend Jo, and recited a very special verse for Jo:

> "Thy words were found,
>   and I did eat them,
>   and Thy word was unto me
>   the joy and rejoicing of my heart,
>   for I am called by Thy name,
>   O Lord God of hosts." (Jer. 15:16)

Then next week Monica began to help Jo learn the verses in Assignment 2—"Pleasing God in My Walk."

And then the other assignments in succeeding weeks:

> Pleasing God in My Talk
> Pleasing God in My Trials
> Pleasing God in My Training
> Pleasing God in My Trusting
> Pleasing God as I Play
> Pleasing God as I Pray
> Pleasing God as I Obey
> Pleasing God as I Work
> Pleasing God as I Witness
> Pleasing God as I Worship

In the twelve week period, Jo had memorized 72 carefully selected Bible verses, arranged under the twelve assignment headings.

As can well be imagined, it was not easy for Jo to do this. Some of his friends in the neighborhood began to make fun of Jo. There were times when Jo rebelled; but Monica, his wise and godly mother, held him to it.

The discipline did not come easy. Satan gave battle also. At times the only thing that enabled Monica to continue this task was through prayer with Jo and the whole family. There were, of course, the other subjects which required time and study, but not the same measure of concentration.

Jo felt greatly rewarded when his loving father commended him and said that he was indeed proud of him.

The pastor of the church where the Augustines attended heard about it and had Jo recite a couple of assignments before the entire congregation. Before long other parents were seeking to find out from Monica how she did it. She explained it to them and told them that one of the things that helped Jo carry on was the book rewards that she was able to present to

Jo along the way. And it was in a church service that she presented to him his completion reward.

The rewards were supplied by the Scripture Memory Fellowship which also provided the Memory Book, "Pleasing God."

The school teacher in charge of any grade can do the same thing with the entire class, adjusting the daily routine, of course, to fit into the hours of the school day and selecting the appropriate book for the grade. Some teachers take two weeks on each assignment.

Objections

At once, some will say, "This is all well and good, but I just don't know how I could do it day after day. I don't know that I can afford that much time and put out that much effort."

My friend, let me tell you this, "You simply cannot afford *not to do it*. You simply must take the time required in order to inscribe the property of the word itself upon the minds of your children. Tutoring your dear child in the word is your most important task. Give it the priority it requires. Their days at home with you pass so quickly, and so do the years. You must plant the word while 'tis day—while you still have them at home and have the opportunity."

Testimony of John Ruskin (1819-1900)

Listen to the testimony of the great Victorian man of letters, John Ruskin, as he reflected upon his training and accomplishments: "All that I have taught of art, everything that I have written, every greatness that has been in any thought of mine, whatever I have done in my life, has simply been due to the fact that when I was a child my mother daily read with me a part of the Bible, and daily made me learn a part of it by heart . . . And truly though I have picked up elements of a little further learning in mathematics, meteorology, and the like in after life—and owe not a little to the teaching of many people—this maternal installation of my mind in that property of the Scriptures, I count very confidently the most precious, and, on the whole, the most essential part of all my education."

An Adult Sunday School Class Memorizing Scripture

Here is a class of fifteen men at the "First" church in Geneva, Illinois. Mr. John Calvin is the capable teacher.

He prayed about the matter. The men seemed to know so little Scripture. He was deeply concerned. He wrote Scripture Memory for help, and secured fifteen copies of the Beginner Adult Series Memory Book 2, titled "Prayer."

The following Sunday, Mr. Calvin handed each man a copy of the book and said, "Brethren, we are going to redeem the time and memorize Scripture, and we'll do it right here. We will begin with assignment one in this book, which is titled, 'Preparation for Prayer.' There are three Bible verses in it—Psalm 66: 18 and Psalm 139:23-24.

"First, we will ask the Lord to help us filter out all distractions and enable us to concentrate on the word.

"The first verse is Psalm 66:18: 'If I regard iniquity in my heart, the Lord will not hear me.'

"Now we will go around and have each man read the verse. By the time we have read it fifteen times, we should be able to remember it, and we will go around again and attempt to recite it. We are all slow learners, so no one will be embarrassed. We will do the best we can."

Implanting the property of Scripture is on the way!

Won't some of the brethren be surprised to be able actually to recite a verse of Scripture?

After that, they did the same with the two short verses in Psalm 139:23-24:

"Search me, O God, and know my heart:
try me, and know my thoughts:
And see if there be any wicked way in me,
and lead me in the way everlasting."

Homework assignment: Mr. Calvin asked each man to recite at home the verses each day after the evening meal or at some other set time.

In the evening service, most of the men were present, and when the pastor gave an opportunity for testimonies, these men stood up one after another and recited Scripture.

John Calvin or the designated person communicated with the absent members and kept them on track. Of course, each man took the Memory Book with him so he could memorize and review the verses at home or at odd times at work during the week.

The following Sunday, Mr. Calvin took assignment two and they learned the three verses on the "Purpose of Prayer." They continued this for fifteen weeks.

In the fifteen weeks, the men learned the fifteen assignments in the book on Prayer and knew a total of some thirty-five Bible verses.

That may be more than some have learned in the last fifteen years.

And who is there that needs the word in mind and heart more than the head of the home—who toils to make a living and who leads the household?

Some problems may arise in such an effort, and they will have to be handled thoughtfully and prayerfully just as other problems are handled.

The Influence Spreads

Phil Melanchthon, a member of Mr. Calvin's Sunday School class, began memorizing with enthusiasm, taking his memory book to work, as Mr. Calvin had suggested.

On Monday, after finishing lunch, he took out his memory book and began concentrating on the first assignment. John Tauler, an employee from another department, noticed the little book Mr. Melanchthon was using as he sat in the cafeteria.

"I see the title of that book you are reading is 'Prayer.' Are you a Christian?"

Mr. Melanchthon was eager to give witness of his faith and asked Mr. Tauler if he wouldn't mind eating lunch at his table so he could try to recite the first verse.

"You know," Mr. Tauler said, "I've been a Christian for several years now, but I've always had trouble memorizing Scripture. Is there any way I can get involved in this?"

Mr. Melanchthon answered, "I don't see why not. In fact, we could use our lunch time to review and discuss these verses each day."

The following Monday, both Mr. Melanchthon and Mr. Tauler were sharing with each other the blessings they had received during the previous week as they worked on their verses. As they sat in the cafeteria, an employee from another department slowed down as he passed their table and remarked, "I see that the title of the booklets you have is 'Prayer.' Are you two Christians?"

And so on it went.

A very unusual thing happened one day when Marty Luther, a salesman for the company who worked out of Wittenberg, Missouri, saw the two men working on their verses. Marty was a Sunday School teacher of a fourth grade class of boys. He told Mr. Melanchthon and Mr. Tauler that he was discouraged with the lack of interest in the Bible shown by the boys. He couldn't help but notice that before class, his boys could recite E.R.A.'s, R.B.I.'s—batting averages, slugging percentages, etc.—with relative ease, but when it came to hiding God's precious word in their hearts, there was little, if any enthusiasm.

"What can I do?" he asked almost in despair.

The two men shared their information about the program of the Scripture Memory Fellowship with great enthusiasm. "They not only have select verses contained in attractive, graded books, but Scripture Memory also gives substantial rewards for successful memorizers."

Marty Luther was deeply interested and secured all the materials from Scripture Memory Fellowship in St. Louis on his way back to Wittenberg, Missouri.

He prepared prayerfully for the opportunity of presenting this "new" method of memorizing to his boys.

After the lesson, Mr. Luther said, "I want to take the last five minutes of our class time to tell you about a program for memorizing Scripture." Those words got the "ho-hum" response he was expecting, so Mr. Luther proceeded, "Those who enroll get to select three progress rewards and one completion reward from this long list of choices." When Mr. Luther opened the Scripture Memory Digest and showed the reward selections, the enthusiasm swelled.

"Now, who would like to take the enrollment form home along with the reward list to show to his mom and dad?" Every hand shot up, but David had a questioning look on his face.

"What's the matter David, aren't you interested in signing up?"

"Sure I am, Mr. Luther, but if it's all right, may I have two of those Digests? I think my sister would like to do this also."

And this goes on and on.

The interest in memorizing Scripture is developed on a one-on-one basis.

Those who are blessed by it are quick to tell others.

What do you think would happen if the pastor had the whole congregation to memorize and recite Scripture in a similar way on Sunday night? The pastor could fill in the commentary and illustrate the meaning and the usefulness of the Scriptures.

Billy Graham, "the prophet with honor," says over and over again, if I could do my life over again, I would memorize more Scripture.

Ken Taylor, whose ambition has been to help people understand the Scriptures, says, "I wish I had memorized more Scripture."

Paul writes his final letter to his closest friend and associate in the work of the Gospel, and says to him in essence, you have known the Scriptures since you were a babe. Your faithful mother, Eunice, and grandmother, Lois, worked with you and implanted the word in your mind and heart—"Continue thou in the things which thou hast learned . . ." The Scripture makes a person "wise unto salvation." "All Scripture is given by inspiration of God, and is profitable for doctrine, for reproof, for correction, for instruction in righteousness" (2 Tim. 3:14-16).

Timothy, oh dear Timothy, *"preach the word."*

And it seems to me I can almost hear the apostle saying, "And take time to instruct the young and the old to 'Eat the good.' "

8

Children

Hearing a young child recite Scripture is the sweetest music this side of heaven.

Almost instinctively every adult knows that the Scripture in the child's heart will exert an immeasurable influence all through life.

Hearing six-year-old *Christopher Hackett* recite with expression the entire book of Galatians is a profound blessing!

The memory is as vivid as if I had heard it just last summer, but it was forty-seven years ago that I heard *Mary Ellen McCarter*, five years of age, recite perfectly the entire High School Memory Book 1 at our camp in Louisiana. This was a total of 250 Bible verses and references organized under twelve assignment topics. The blessing of that occasion lingers to this day, and I can only imagine what a powerful influence those Scriptures have been in her life and how Mary Ellen, now 52 years of age, is still relishing the sweetness of those words which she laid up in her heart before she really understood what they meant.

Should Young Children Memorize Scripture?

There are indeed certain "authorities" even in evangelical circles today who proclaim that memorizing Scripture is not desirable for young children because the truth is not understood and is not related to the child's experience. Consequently, they say, it has no value.

But actual experience and the *authority* of the Scriptures flatly contradict such a conclusion. Many parents all over the land speak favorably about the value and blessing of having their young chldren memorizing God's word. There are scores of such testimonies from parents at the home schooling conventions in different places.

The Apostle Paul specifically reminds Timothy, that "from a child thou hast known the holy Scriptures" (2 Tim. 3:15). The word for child here is *brephos* and means, "infant, babe, babbler." We have also the revealing instruction in Isaiah which tells us that doctrine and Scripture are to be the diet even of babes: "Whom shall he teach knowledge? and to whom shall he make to understand doctrine? Them that are weaned from the milk, and drawn from the breasts. For precept must be upon precept, precept upon precept; line upon line, line upon line; here a little, and there a little" (Isa. 28:9-10).

Little by little, impressions are made by the word of God in the experience of the children, "as the Spirit opens their understanding." First comes the light for the new birth, and then more light for growth in character and service. The days and nights, the months, the seasons come and go, and during all that time there continues the learning, the remembering, the reciting and the gradual understanding of what God has revealed in His word.

In the very first instruction in the Bible concerning

storing God's word in the heart, we read, "These words, which I command thee this day, shall be in thine heart: and thou shalt teach them diligently to thy children . . ." (Deut. 6:6-7). This is a strong directive from God, and teaching children to remember Scripture is indeed a big job.

But we must give the little ones prior attention in this respect. If difficulties arise in the process due to the child's immaturity and levity of mind, they are more than balanced by the child's freedom from the prejudices and the perplexing cares of life that hinder the adult from taking in God's word. Little children instinctively desire to penetrate the unknown; they seize upon explanations about God and nature with eagerness; they accept the revelation of God and the explanation of parent or teacher with trusting confidence.

If objections are raised that children cannot grasp the meaning of Scripture, we should remember that at no stage of life can man comprehend the things of God (1 Cor. 2:14). At every level of human experience, it takes the illuminating work of the Holy Spirit to learn spiritual truth and "to know the things that are freely given to us of God" (1 Cor. 2:12).

We are often quite amazed at how early in life little children seem to get at the meaning of Scripture, and are able to apply it in everyday situations. *Mrs. R. D. Robinson, Texas*, told a humorous story of how their five year old boy used one of the verses he had memorized on his "growling" kitten: "This new ABC plan is just marvelous," she said, "Our youngest memorized it last year. He even used some of the Scripture on his kitten, which growled a lot one morning. Philip said in a very determined voice, 'K . . . Keep thy tongue from evil.' We were all amazed that he could not only remember the verse, but be able to apply it to a home situation."

What It Takes

What does it really take to get our children —young and older—to memorize Scripture?

It all begins with the parent, the teacher and the pastor. There must be an unwavering conviction on the part of those who would instruct the children that implanting God's word in the heart of the young is not only important but that it is absolutely imperative. Reading Bible stories to them and giving them a general knowledge of the Bible is good, but it is not enough. We must implant—instill—the property of the word itself. They need to have God's own words stored in their memory. What God has said must be clearly and accurately engraved upon their hearts. David understood this when he said, "Thy word have I hid in my heart, that I might not sin against Thee" . . . It is "a lamp unto my feet and a light unto my path" (Ps. 119:11, 105).

What is the responsiveness of the average child or young person to the idea of assimilating the Holy Scriptures? The preschool and elementary grade child takes in the words eagerly, but when he passes through adolescence and as he grows older, he begins to evaluate things for himself. He does not see how the Bible fits into his general education nor how it will help him to earn a living. When he has free time, his natural inclinations generally dominate his activities. Play, sports, the tube and just idling time away with a friend or two is preferable to the discipline involved in memorizing something which the parents happen to believe is so very good for him. Given an option, the average child will reach for the comic book instead of the Bible memory book. It is not that the young person is necessarily rebellious or intent upon an evil course, but it seems unusually difficult for him to be steadily enthusiastic about spiritual objectives.

But the heart of the problem involves much more.

The whole world system is set against the person who purposes to advance spiritually. Satan, who controls this world's program, applies the pressures where they will hurt the most. As soon as the young lad or girl wholeheartedly begins to read, study and memorize the word, there will at once come opposition, ridicule, persecution and a wide variety of subtle attacks.

Let's face it. Satan does not want our children to store up God's word, and he can always be counted upon to give battle. It becomes an intense spiritual warfare. Thank God that "greater is He that is in you than he that is in the world." The Lord is on our side, and victory is assured.

So what do we do, then, in getting them to memorize Scripture?

Say

Yes, *say* it. Just tell your children that they are going to memorize Scripture. Command them. *Make* them do it, just like you make them do many other things. After all, you *are* the parent.

John Ruskin's mother *made* her son memorize the Scriptures.

She made him memorize God's word by virtue of her parental authority. She persisted with it day after day and year after year because she loved her son and because she was his mother. *John Ruskin* (1819-1900) says in his autobiography, "As soon as I was able to read with fluency, she began a course of Bible work with me, which never ceased till I went to Oxford."

Compelling a child to pursue and accomplish a desirable task involves much more than just a "crack of the whip." Every mother knows this and so do most of the teachers.

Remember the Scripture in Deuteronomy 6:6-7? "These words which I command thee this day shall be in thine heart, and thou shalt teach them *diligently* unto thy children . . ." (emphasis mine) But the verse continues, "And shalt talk of them when thou sittest in thine house, and when thou walkest by the way, and when thou liest down, and when thou risest up."

This is very interesting. You shall "talk" about those Scriptures, explain them, help the child to understand them and appreciate them. Yes, talk of them when you are sitting around the house, talk of them when you are out walking leisurely, or when you are on some errand, reflect upon the Scriptures at bedtime, when you pray together, talk of them as soon as you arise and commit your way unto the Lord. All through the day, week after week, and year after year, you persist, you persevere with the basic job of tutoring the young mind in the eternal verities of God! That's it. It comes only as a direct result of deliberate effort—sustained effort, unceasing effort.

Procrastination is an elusive thief when it comes to utilizing our time. The wise parent or teacher will follow undeviatingly a set schedule for learning and for reciting. If left to himself, the child's repeated procrastinations soon erode whatever interest has been achieved. This leads to discouragement and frustration. Sit down with the young scholar and together carefully set up the daily schedule. John Ruskin remembered many years later that the first thing after breakfast was set apart for reading the Bible and memorizing portions of it and that "no interruptions from servants were allowed, nor from visitors, who either joined in the reading or waited."

The child will try all sorts of schemes to get you to ease up on the requirements. He will argue with you. He will fight back at you. He will resist. He may weep and stomp his feet and say some hard things like, "I am not going to do it. I don't like the Bible! You are going to make me hate it all my life." Yes, he will say such things and almost drive you to distraction, and certainly to your knees, but then ere long he will come back and say so sweetly, "I am so glad you *made* me learn those verses."

Play

We must not overlook the "play" instinct of children, and endeavor as much as possible to make Bible learning enjoyable to them. It is really "fun" of the highest calibre to examine and to acquire the very words which the almighty God has spoken.

Mark Twain said that Helen Keller was one of the two most interesting characters of the nineteenth century—the other was Napoleon. While still in her young years, someone asked her if she liked to study.

"Yes," she replied, "but I like to play also, and I feel sometimes as if I were a music box with all play shut up inside me."

Are not almost all children that way?

Are not even adults inclined in that direction?

"And that from a child, thou hast known the holy Scriptures," Paul said to Timothy. The words that are rendered "holy Scriptures" are uncommon and carry the idea of "sacred writings" or "sacred letters." Dear old grandmother Lois or the beloved mother Eunice might have held tiny Tim on her knee, taken his little finger and traced out certain letters of Bible words, and given him the "feel" of the Scripture scrolls. Timothy learned his ABCs from the Bible. We can imagine the mother starting out with the first letter of the alphabet (*Aleph* in Hebrew and *Alpha* in Greek) and telling the infant the name of the first man, ADAM. She would not lecture him, but *play* with a purpose.

She would make certain that the child enjoyed it and be content for him to learn very slowly—letter after letter, letter after letter, line upon line, line upon line.

Finally, it might lead to a flash card that looked like this:

A   bel
D   avid
A   braham
M   oses

How exciting to learn about the first man and his son Abel. Then the mother and grandmother would tell their Timothy about *David*. Later he would find out that it was David who wrote many of the Psalms. With *Abraham*, they would plant the first thoughts about the beginning of the Hebrew nation. And then it was *Moses* who led them out of Egypt.

Eunice and Lois played the "Bible game" with Timothy in teaching him to understand and memorize the word. For the small child it is play; for the wise mother it is astute pedagogy. Their plan worked, and Timothy learned not just things *about* the Bible, but he imbibed the property of the Scriptures themselves from the time he was a babe.

The Apostle Paul commends Timothy's mother and grandmother (2 Tim. 1:5), and charges Timothy not to forget his early training, "But continue thou in the things which thou hast learned and hast been assured of, knowing of whom thou hast learned them" (2 Tim. 3:14).

"Play" the Bible game with the little ones. Do it in love. Let them learn the ABC letters through use of the Bible. This is so much more desirable than the practice of so many in our day who use primers that are filled with secular matter and who put off the "sacred letters" until later years, which too often never seem to come.

This was the case in the training of the liberal philosopher, *John Stuart Mill* (1806-1873), whose father proceeded on the fallacious principle that a religious upbringing would interfere with a free development, and withheld all Bible teaching from the boy until he could form an "unbiased judgment" on the "subject of religion." The result was that his brilliant son never did get out of the morass of rationalism.

Remember that while the truth of God's word is being withheld until a mature judgment can be formed, the mind does not remain in a vacuum, but is all that time being subjected to the wiles of the devil who fills the mind with "tares" and causes it to become warped and prejudiced against the things of God. Remember also the principle that *Francis Bacon* enunciated centuries ago, "Things alter for the worse spontaneously if they do not alter for the better designedly."

Nothing makes so lasting an impression on the tender young mind as the word of God.

Present God's word to the little ones in an attractive way. Make it a "fun" learning. *Barbara Lockwood,* who memorized in our system while she was growing up, developed a book of a hundred "Fun Ideas" for Bible memory. It is published by Standard, Cincinnati.

In this respect, many parents and teachers have found the children's Bible memorizing materials of the *Scripture Memory Fellowship* very appealing. The "I AM Memory Book" and the "ABC Memory Book" for the preschool children are delightful. Young children find them irresistible. Yes, let them handle these books. Play with them. Eunice and Lois would probably have allowed baby Tim to handle them as he would, right side up and upside down, and even chew on them a bit if he liked. All the time he would be "eating" the solid food of the Scripture as he learned his ABCs.

Why do we learn the ABCs anyway? Well, the average person would probably answer, "We learn them so we can know how to read, write and be intelligent." But why learn to read and be intelligent? Such a question provokes many answers depending on the ambitions of each person. We believe that Paul and Timothy would say, "We learn the ABCs so that we may know how to read and memorize the word of God and become enlightened on how to be saved and how to grow in grace."

While the child's mind is like a shallow, rippling brook which dances over the stony path of its education and in its movement touches here a flower, there a bush and then in the occasional placid flow it reflects the fleecy cloud above, thank God for the parents and teachers with loving tact and dedicated genius who seize upon the happy mood of the child, and without crushing the "music box" instinct, guide the young learner's thoughts into the depth and breadth of the broadening river of eternal truth.

Pay

Read again chapter six on the "Incentives."

Yes, "pay" them to memorize Scripture.

It is strange that not a single word spoken by Timothy is recorded in the New Testament.

But I can imagine him saying, "I thank God for my mother and grandmother who patiently taught me to memorize God's word. I remember the special treats for memorizing Scripture. I remember their loving words of encouragement. I will never forget the Apostle Paul's commendation, and how he exhorted me 'to continue' and never stop memorizing and meditating on the Scriptures. God's word itself is my abiding reward. It is by the word of the living God that I can 'be strong in the grace that is in Christ Jesus . . . endure hardness as a good soldier of Jesus Christ . . . be an example of the believers . . . and preach the word in season and out of season.' "

Pray

When all else seems to fail, seek the face of God in earnest intercessions. Pray for them by name; pray with them; God surely loves to hear such prayers because it is God who "commands" us to lay up His word in our hearts (Deut. 11:18).

"Robert was a dunce."

The children in school first began to say it; the neighbors began to repeat it; even his own parents began to think it. Robert was a *dunce*, just too stupid to learn. The boy hated to go to school and the teachers hated to see him come.

But his father and mother were true Christians, and they began to pray for Robert.

Every morning the father took down the family Bible and read a portion from it, and then they prayed as a family.

Somehow, Robert's parents recognized that Robert's problem was a spiritual one. They could see that there was a strange barrier to learning. They prayed for their son. They also prayed with him. Although the community rather casually dismissed the boy as a dunce, the parents loved their son and they just could not give up.

Then one day they said to him, "Robert, we want you to memorize Scripture, and we will work with you. We believe it will help you in many ways."

Robert was not too enthused about it, but seeing how intent his parents were for his sake, he consented. Many a day, Robert sat with his Bible open committing to memory the verses that were assigned to him. Often he longed to shut the book and run outside to join his companions in their games, but his mother held him to the task. When he seemed inclined to rebel, she prayed with him.

The young boy sensed the deep love with which

his parents prevailed upon him to memorize the verses.

At the age of twelve, Robert stood before the whole congregation in the Presbyterian church and recited Psalm 119—all 176 verses.

The people went home saying, "That boy is not such a dunce after all."

Robert accepted the Lord Jesus Christ as Savior soon after he began memorizing the Scriptures, and turned over his life to God for whatever service God desired for him.

The "dunce" came alive. His grades in school improved dramatically. His father and mother were now praising the Lord as well as praying.

In the year 1807, Robert sailed for China, as the very first missionary to that land. Before he could do any work as a missionary, he first had to learn the language. It was very difficult. Someone said that "to learn Chinese you must have lungs of steel, a head of oak, eyes of an eagle, memory of angels, and the life-span of Methuselah."

Again, God answered prayer. Robert learned the language so that he could speak it like a Chinese person. He translated the Bible into that language, and with the help of others, he developed an English-Chinese dictionary in six volumes.

Today that boy who was known as a dunce is remembered as *Robert Morrison* (1782-1834), pioneer missionary, who did a work for the Lord in China that has probably never been equaled.

How then do we get the children to memorize Scripture? Well, we don't just hand them the memory book and say "Here is your book—now get busy and memorize!"

We recognize that we are undertaking the teaching of the greatest subject in the universe. It embraces the greatest potential. It involves the eternal destinies of our children.

We persist day after day. Even with the most rebellious or the most handicapped children committed to our care, we do not give up. We seek the strength and the blessing of God who gave us the word. We can count very heavily upon His faithfulness to answer prayer. He is deeply involved in this subject inasmuch as He Himself has "commanded" us to have His words in our hearts and to "teach them diligently" to our children.

To A Mother

No greater thing can any mother give
To any child than this great glorious truth,
Foundation on which lives may build and live!
Oh, lay the rock of faith while there is youth!
So swift the years will carry them away.
Beyond your reaching hands, your voice's call!
Give them the things they cannot lose, today.
Give them the Word, the greatest gift of all.

—Grace Noll Crowell

9

Understanding

"Understandest thou what thou readest?" was the appropriate question Philip asked of the Ethiopian, riding in the chariot and reading the prophecy of Isaiah (Acts 8:30).

Now, here you are reading a Scripture which you are intent on committing to memory. Do you understand it? A clear and distinct apprehension is necessary in order for it to stick and dwell in your memory. Sink deeply into your mind the meaning of it. Lay hold of the thoughts contained in the Scripture. Therefore, you will be placing in your memory not just words but the thoughts expressed by those words.

Clear perception of the meaning enables your memory to take hold of it. A faint glimmering of the thoughts will vanish like images seen in twilight.

Nehemiah records an interesting detail in connection with the rebuilding of the temple in Jerusalem by the Jewish remnant from Babylon. He tells how "Ezra the scribe stood upon a pulpit of wood, which they had made for that purpose" (Neh. 8:4) and read the Scriptures to the people. The record goes on—"So they read in the book in the law of God distinctly, and gave the sense, and caused them to understand the reading" (Neh. 8:8). Understanding the Scripture prepares the way for assimilating it.

It is very difficult—if not impossible—to retain and recall what we do not understand. When the meaning of the passage is clearly understood, you proceed to memorize it, taking in the whole passage or at least a complete sentence. You do not set out to memorize single words or phrases.

A good many years ago, I went to a restaurant with a group of young people after the evening service in our church. Among them was George, who was about twenty-three years of age. He was mentally retarded and probably never went beyond grade three.

Most of them had enrolled in the Basic Adult plan, which calls for memorizing seven verses per week. I asked them how they were doing. Some of them were behind and began to make excuses. When George's turn came, he reported joyfully that he had completed the assignment, and his "hearer," who was also present, confirmed the fact, and stated that he did it perfectly.

I asked George to tell us how he did it. He proceeded enthusiastically somewhat as follows: "The way I do it is start with the first word and repeat it over and over again until I know it for sure. Then I take the next word and repeat it many times along with the first word. I take one word at a time until I have memorized the whole verse."

His diligence is certainly commendable, but he was doing it the hard way. He was simply memorizing words instead of thoughts.

You must first seek to understand the meaning of the verse as clearly as possible. That's the reason why our memory books have the verses arranged under a particular topic, and then explanatory notes are supplied at the bottom of the page. Study the notes. Study what the commentaries have to say, if such are accessible. Read the passage in its context in your Bible. Compare the words or phrases of that verse with similar words in other Bible passages. Since we believe that the Holy Spirit is the Supreme Author in the writing of *all* Scriptures, it follows then that "Scripture is the best interpreter of Scripture."

The Holy Spirit indwells the believer the moment he is saved (1 Cor. 6:19). This means that the most distinguished private Tutor takes up residence in each believer (1 Jn. 2:27). He is the One who "will guide you into all truth" (Jn. 16:13). He will unlock and unfold the sacred mysteries of God, "yea, the deep things of God" (1 Cor. 2:10). He has intimate knowledge of *all* things, *all* truth, *all* events, *all* beings. He delights to open our understanding that we might more fully know and glorify our Lord Jesus Christ (Jn. 16:13-14).

One of the most concise, yet complete statements dealing with the understanding of divine truth is found in *Myles Coverdale's Rules for Reading the Bible* (1535). Addressing the reader in his prologue, he wrote:

> "It shall greatly help you
> to understande Scripture,
> if thou mark not only
> what is spoken or wrytten,
> but of whom and to whom,
> with what words,
> at what time, where,
> to what intent,
> with what circumstances,
> considering what goeth before
> and what followeth."

Another requisite in understanding the word of God is prompt obedience. "I understand more than the ancients," David declared, "because I keep Thy precepts" (Ps. 119:100). *Oswald Chambers* (1874-1917), author of the classic devotional book, "My Utmost for His Highest," strongly emphasizes this point: "The tiniest fragment of obedience, and heaven opens and the profoundest truths of God are yours straight away."

David prayed, "Open Thou my eyes that I may behold wondrous things out of Thy law" (Ps. 119:18), and in the same Psalm he pleads five times for "understanding": "Give me understanding, and I shall keep Thy law" (34); "Give me understanding, that I may learn Thy commandments" (73); "Give me understanding, that I may know Thy testimonies" (125); "Give me understanding, and I shall live" (144); "Give me understanding according to Thy word" (169).

Therefore, in undertaking to memorize Scripture, we read it thoughtfully, we study it, taking in the notes which are supplied and consulting other explanatory works, and we earnestly seek the illumination of the Holy Spirit in prayer. We do these things in order to *understand* what we desire to commit to memory.

"What we do not understand, we do not possess."

10

Concentration

Concentration is the art of thinking attentively.

Concentrating on the Scriptures is the employment of that art for maximum gain.

Concentration is the God-given power of being able to learn and retain what has been learned so that it can be recalled in the days and months to come.

Concentration is the backbone, the sustaining factor in memorization. You can be reading or studying the Scriptures while your mind wanders off and you find yourself going back to yesterday's problems or jumping ahead and tackling tomorrow's schedule. When you are memorizing the word, however, you definitely have to exclude everything else and give it undivided attention. *Mrs. E. Hosbach, Michigan*, has found to be true what most of us have experienced again and again. "Often," she said, "I find myself allowing cares and perplexities to fill my mind, but when I am learning these verses, such things are crowded out."

An unoccupied mind does not stay in neutral. It is generally plagued with cares, worries, bitter thoughts, vain regrets and a whole jumble of unprofitable musings. Place your mind in the first gear—exercise that controlled attention long enough for the distractions to be filtered out. Woo your brain into concentrating. Think attentively upon the meaning of the Scripture you are trying to lock in your memory. If your mind wanders, bring it back quickly to that Scripture.

There are many, well-meaning people who keep searching for some system whereby they could memorize Scripture without having to concentrate. There are also some promoters who indirectly promise such a plan. But there is no shortcut to memorizing Scripture or anything else. There is no magical formula. In order to commit Scripture to memory, you must *do* something. There is no way of getting inside the brain and turning on some switches and thereby instantly committing things to memory. You may visualize, organize and vocalize, but then you must do something. You have to make an expenditure of mental energy. You have to think attentively. You have to *concentrate.*

Having a tape recorder playing the Scripture while you sleep does not work. It places nothing in your conscious memory. It is a profitless fantasy.

Do not keep delaying. Do not fight concentration. Engage your mind—first, second and third gear—and lay hold of the prize!

Memorizing Scripture calls for real effort, but it produces rich dividends in every area of life.

Eye-minded or Ear-minded

Our senses are the means of perception. We perceive and get at information by the senses: seeing, hearing, touching, tasting and smelling. The most important are seeing and hearing.

Distinguish between the eye-minded and the ear-minded persons. People are eye-minded if they remember best the things as a result of seeing—seeing the print or realistic pictures that suggest the thought in that print. Those who are ear-minded remember best the things which they hear—in their own voice or that of somebody else.

If you are eye-minded, you learn best by reading the verse of Scripture in your Bible or memory book. You would also be inclined to receive significant help from seeing illustrations of the thoughts in that verse.

If you are ear-minded, you benefit more from hearing that verse of Scripture, and particularly if you hear it spoken in your own voice. This is why some people dictate the passage of Scripture on a cassette tape, and then listen to it.

Having said this, it is well to realize that most people are not exclusively eye-minded or ear-minded. Generally, we utilize both senses and may not be aware as to which sense serves us best.

It is well to remember a word from our Creator: "The hearing ear and the seeing eye, the Lord hath made even both of them" (Prov. 20:12), and the same Lord can tune them both to receive His word.

Evening Sleeper or Morning Sleeper

It might be of some value to pass on what observers in this field have learned regarding the best time to memorize. They classify people into two broad categories: "evening sleeper" and "morning sleeper." Generally speaking, the evening sleepers learn and memorize best in the morning. The opposite, of course, holds true for the morning sleepers. They are wide awake by the afternoon, and the evening hours are the best time to focus close attention on the passage of God's precious word they desire to file in their memory.

Some of us are both evening and morning sleepers,

but let not that be taken as an excuse for not memorizing the word of Him who "giveth His beloved sleep" (Ps. 127:2).

The Value

The object of all Scripture memorization is twofold: (1) To enjoy and profit from the very process of placing the holy words of God into the storage bins of the brain. (2) To have the verses instantly accessible for use in any opportunity for witness and in every time of personal need. The memory retention will increase in proportion to the time spent in review — particularly a review in the actual use of those Scriptures. Appropriating the Scriptures in our efforts to be obedient to the will of God will greatly facilitate our ability to retain them. Then there is the blessing of being able to meditate on the word—day and night.

Most Christians recognize not only the value of memorizing God's word but they also see how essential it is in the believer's life and service. They will readily admit this, but probably the main reason why they do not pursue it more diligently is because it involves work—determination, discipline and the investment of mental energy.

Learning to concentrate means acquiring a tremendous skill which will stand us in good stead no matter what our vocation in life becomes. Concentrating on God's word will result in spiritual blessing and prosperity all the days of our life (Josh. 1:8). Young people who memorize prescribed portions of Scripture year after year generally discover that this becomes a great asset in high school and college; and the word, made readily accessible, makes their witness for the Lord spontaneous and effectual.

More than likely, you value and appreciate the word of God. You are probably also keenly aware of the fact that you need to memorize it so that it will be instantly accessible in every moment of need.

Butterfly or Bee

Therefore, take time, slow down and concentrate —think attentively—upon these rich treasures given to us by God.

Consider the flowers in gardens and fields and the visitors they attract. Among the insects which subsist on the sweet nectar of flowers, there are two very different kinds. You have probably noticed them.

One is remarkable for its brilliant wings, which sparkle like gems in the sunlight. As you watch its jaunty gyrations over the fields, you cannot help admiring the graceful activity. It dances from flower to flower, sips elegantly the ready nectar wherever it can easily be found, and really gets over the entire field.

There is another "worker" in the same field whose simple attire and business-like flight may not have attracted much attention. This diligent plodder does not overlook any flower, and wherever it alights, it generally finds nectar. If the flower-cup be deep, it goes down to the bottom; if the dragon-mouth be shut, it thrusts its lips asunder and explores its luscious recesses. Its rival of the "painted velvet wing," has no patience for such dull and time-consuming effort.

But what is the end of all the activity? Why, the butterfly died last October along with the flowers; the bee is warm in his hive amidst the fragrant stores which he gathered during the summer!

Now, to which class do you belong—the butterfly or the bee?

Do you just flit along and look for something easy and novel, or do you seriously ponder the Scriptures? Have you been taking time in the generous sunlight of the day to concentrate on the word of God and place it in your memory?

Does the word dwell richly in your heart, so that in the solitude of a sick room, in the vigils of a restless night, in the winter of old age, or in the desolation of unexpected mental impoverishment, the stored-up divine words of comfort perpetuate summer round about you, and give you meat to eat that the world knows nothing about?

11

Strategies

There are certain strategies and techniques that have helped people to learn and to retain Scripture. It is well to consider them since they have been of value to others. Each memorizer, however, will likely adapt the methods suggested, or he will come up with his own techniques.

As you approach the memorization of Scripture, allow yourself to become fascinated anew by its very excellence and captivated by the practical value it has for you.

The process of memorizing Scripture will be greatly affected by the *value* you place on it, the *energy* you reserve for it, the quality *time* you allow for it, and the degree of *delight* with which you pursue it.

Seek out a quiet place as much as possible. Shut off the radio, the TV, and disallow other disturbances. Seek the Lord in prayer and ask Him to filter out the many cares and responsibilities that are on your mind.

(1) *Associations:* As you ponder the meaning of the Scripture, strive to form as many associations as possible with what you already know. Impressions

are not stored away in isolated compartments. Remembering becomes a network of connections so that one thing serves to remind you of another. One writer states that, "We can remember a new idea only by connecting it with something we already know." Supposing you are trying to learn Psalm 27:1, "The Lord is my light and my salvation; whom shall I fear?" You at once associate it with the dark night when you were afraid, or it may connect with Psalm 56:3, "What time I am afraid, I will trust in Thee."

(2) *Letter Associations:* One of the oldest and most effective methods of association is to use the first letter of key words, and combine them into a single word, phrase or sentence. For example, in learning Philippians 4:8, you may find it difficult to remember the order of things to think upon—"Finally brethren, whatsoever things are *true,* whatsoever things are *honest,* whatsoever things are *just,* whatsoever things are *pure,* whatsoever things are *lovely,* whatsoever things are of good *report,* if there be any virtue and if there be any praise, think on these things." It becomes easier to remember them if you will take the first letter from each of the significant words and let it become the first letter of each word in a sentence like this: *Tomorrow, have Jim put linens right.*

To remember the names of the five Great Lakes, you think of HOMES (Huron, Ontario, Michigan, Erie, Superior). Or, you may invent a word like VIBGYOR to remember the order of the colors formed by the sun in a rainbow, namely, violet, indigo, blue, green, yellow, orange and red. Letter associations can be utilized effectively for remembering a difficult series of words in Scripture.

(3) *Other Connections:* Connect with each passage of Scripture, or with each assignment, a room in your

house, or a piece of furniture, or a certain food, or some person, or a certain kind of weather. The more connections you form with the particular Scripture you are endeavoring to memorize, the better. I remember the first assignment in Basic Adult book four, and particularly Colossians 1:16-17—"For by Him were all things created . . ." because I was memorizing it while in the diner of the Union Pacific train and traveling through the massive Rocky Mountains going out west. This took place about thirty-five years ago. The closer you can approximate the context in which something was learned, the more likely you will be able to recall it.

(4) *Context:* Look up in the Bible the verse you are seeking to learn, and read it in its context. Underline it in your Bible. Trying to recall the context of the verse helps to zero in on the particular verse.

(5) *Writing: Isaac Watts* (1674-1748), father of English hymnody, states in his great essay on "The Improvement of the Mind," that "Once writing over what we desire to remember and giving due attention to what we write, will fix it more in the mind than reading it five times." This is probably most effective for the folk who remember best what they can see instead of what they hear.

> "Sounds which address the ear are lost and die
> In one short hour; but that which strikes the eye
> Lives long upon the mind; the faithful sight
> Engraves the knowledge with a beam of light."

(6) *Recording:* Record the Scriptures on a cassette, and then listen while driving, or while at home or office. There is something about hearing it in your own voice, as previously suggested, that helps the memory, especially if the reading was done thought-

fully and with correct expression.

(7) *Singing:* Select the melody of a familiar hymn or chorus that will suit the words of the Scripture, or make up a singable melody. This becomes a great help, particularly for children and young people. Remember Psalm 89:1—"I will sing of the mercies of the Lord for ever . . ."

(8) *Avoid Crowding:* Do not force yourself in trying to master the whole passage at one time. Be satisfied if some of the key words begin to stick. Allow them to sink in your memory, and after an interval of an hour or two or even a day, come back to it with fresh vigor. Better work is done in short periods of time, with breaks for reflection.

(9) *Try Reciting:* First you read the Scripture a few times. But then you must try reciting. This is what really engages the memory, and where concentration begins. Do not be afraid to trust your memory. See how much you can say without looking on the page. Attempting to recite calls for mental energy and is vital in learning the verses.

(10) *Relax:* Don't be anxious about getting through with the memorizing quickly. Relax and enjoy God's thoughts concerning you. You don't have anything better to do—do you? Relish words spoken by God, and let them minister grace to your heart.

(11) *Whole Learning* is generally considered more efficient than "part learning." Read the entire assignment or passage carefully several times. You may then prefer to concentrate on one verse or sentence. After the framework of the main thoughts has emerged, the details will follow more easily. "Visualize the whole, then execute the parts."

(12) *Overlearn* the verses. This means putting a little extra time on them after you already know them. This will help to seal the Scripture in your memory.

(13) *Harness Reminders:* Let the digital clock remind you of Scripture references—especially at night when your mind is not pursuing anything else intently. Look at the clock; it says 12:02, and that brings to mind Hebrews 12:2. While driving, look at the license plate numbers. Just ahead of you is Missouri JAS 122. Why, that's James 1:22!

(14) *Redeem Time:* Redeem the time that is normally wasted or not fully utilized. Have the verses before you while shaving, while quilting, while washing dishes, while riding, while sitting in the doctor's office, while walking or cycling. Or you can just engage in rapid review by running the verses through your mind.

(15) *Fellowship:* Get together with other memorizers for an hour or an evening. In North Carolina, Steve and Alicia Rehburg meet with Ross and Karen Hall—children included—for an evening of fellowship in reciting and discussing their Bible verses. My son Jim met with his friend Peter Geisz regularly. They recited their verses and discussed the meaning. When they separated for university, they continued, on a less regular basis, to hold each other accountable over the telephone. Responsibility to a friend motivates the discipline needed in systematic memorization.

(16) *Usage:* Use the verses you have memorized in your meditation while driving, trying to sleep or waiting. Use the verses in conversation, in teaching, and in witnessing. Plant a verse, not win an argument. Usage

is one of the most valuable means of reviewing and retaining what has been memorized.

(17) *Sixth Sense:* And then there is for the believer the spiritual sixth sense, as it were. We learn by the enthusiasm with which we delight in the word. The natural man knows nothing about this. When a person is born again, he receives a new desire whereby, in the exercise of mind and heart, he can taste the blessedness of the words and thoughts of God. Like the psalmist, the saint says, "I will delight myself in Thy statutes; I will not forget Thy word" (119:16), and what do you know, he has the Scripture in memory. The "sixth sense" is difficult to explain, but for the believer in communion with God, it is not difficult to experience.

Sometimes we may feel discouraged about spending so much time in memorizing words written thousands of years ago!

But these are God's words!

In the times in which we live, there is nothing in the whole world so much to be desired as solid words: words of truth; words of love; words expressing infinite love. Treasures, pleasures, plaudits and honors of this world, what are they? My unsatisfied soul cries out, give me words—words whereby I may know the amazing love that God has for me; words which declare the unchangeable faithfulness of the Savior; words purifying my heart, emboldening me in prayer, exhibiting to me the glorious future.

"How sweet are Thy words to my taste! Yea, sweeter than honey to my mouth" (Ps. 119:97-104).

Such a relish for the word will cause *soul-rise* before *sunrise* as in Psalm 119:147—"early, even before the dawning of the morning, did I make supplication: I hoped in Thy word,"—and in the very next verse we see Bible meditation by *star-light*: "Mine eyes anticipate the night watches, to meditate on Thy word"

82

(*Delitzsch*). This is God's plan! Read and memorize the word by day, and in the night watches, when sleep eludes you, muse upon it.

In those night seasons—in those times of dryness and desolation—God's word silently falls on our souls to revive and to prepare us for the trials of the day. "My speech shall distill as the dew," God says, "as the small rain on the tender herb . . ." (Deut. 32:2). Just as the tiny dewdrops revive the little stems of the fading plants with the life-renewing moisture, so God distills His "speech"—His precious nutriment—into our frail spiritual life, or it would quickly wither under the fiery trials and burning heat.

Our minds never sleep, and it's truly amazing how God refreshes our spirits during the hours of sleep when, it seems, the word which we have assimilated previously nourishes our hearts and minds. We do not hear any sound of abundance of rain; our senses are not aroused; we may be too sick or too wearied from the battle and quite unable to *take in* any words; but just the same, midst the spiritual desolation, or in the wilderness journey, God tenderly watches over us and His word—His comforting, His enlivening "speech"—keeps on distilling softly as the dew "and thereby strengthening our hearts and minds through Christ Jesus."

How blessed these truths have been to me during many nights of indescribable anguish and trial! Fighting high fever and weird hallucinations in a foreign land, I could almost hear His gentle footsteps near me! Perhaps this is what the psalmist was enduring when he said, "When I remember Thee upon my bed, and meditate on Thee in the night watches" (63:6).

Whatever strategy, whatever effort it takes, we must, we will assimilate God's words!

12

Mnemonics

In the last thirty years or so, there has been a great deal said about *mnemonics,* particularly by secular writers. Basically, it refers to certain methods of memory enhancement. But nowhere had I seen any explanation as to what the word "mnemonics" really means or why it is being used in reference to memory methods.

A few months ago, while reading in an old volume an article by a seventeenth century writer, I came upon the explanation.

Mnemon was the surname for Artaxerxes II, king of Persia, 404-358 B.C. The word "mnemon" means mindful. From his youth to his old age, *Mnemon* never read anything without making some small points, dashes, or hooks in the margin, to mark what parts of the discourse were desirable for remembering. And when he came to the end of the section or chapter, he sought to recollect all the sentiments or expressions he had marked, so that he could give a tolerable analysis and abstract of the treatise he had just read.

Through the years his name has been taken to describe similar markings and methods in the improvement of memory and recollection.

So much for the meaning of the word *mnemonics*.

Mnemonic devices depend upon the use of some method of coding that which is to be remembered. This may be useful in certain limited fields, especially if the coding is done by the person who will be using it. The use of mnemonics has declined steadily due to the inevitable complexity of the devices.

In 1960, *Mr. O. W. Hayes* declared on the dust jacket of his book, *Your Memory,* "In just seven days, you, too, can be a memory wizard." About the same time, *Mr. Harry Lorayne* advertised his *Instant Memory Course* on an LP recording. Then there were the visual aids for memory instruction put out by *Vicore, Inc.*, whose services were used for a short time by schools and government agencies. However, it was soon abandoned, and its president, *Mrs. Elsie Carlson,* said that their system of mnemonics was "as good as any there is, but," she continued, "it took more time for students to learn the system than it was worth."

Probably the most ambitious undertaking in the realm of mental wizardry was that of *Dr. Bruno Furst.* It appeared on big-time TV shows and was written up in popular magazines. The course sold for $15.75, and basically it offered three systems: (1) The "hook system" which begins by giving you a letter and a word for each figure up to a hundred. (2) The second was the "chain method" where you need not memorize a whole speech but just a chain outline of key words. (3) The third was a "classification system" where you organized what you wanted to remember into categories of things with similarities. Dr. Furst has written books on the subject, and some of them can still be found in city libraries.

In more recent years, much attention has been given to artificial memory-code systems of associations. In 1976, thousands of people—ministers and laymen—flocked to seminars in Los Angeles and elsewhere, where they hoped to learn a simple system of memory by association. The "short cut" seekers were told that pictures are much easier to remember than words. They were shown a series of cartoon images symbolizing phrases and concepts to be remembered. One example featured an illustration of a dove pulling a cross which stood on a loaf of bread. The bread rested on an airplane; all of this was held up by Satan, with horns and forked tail, with a stone in each upraised hand. This, if you please, was to help you fasten in your memory the exact words of Matthew 4:4—"Man shall not live by bread alone, but by every word that proceedeth out of the mouth of God."

What are the conclusions regarding the use of the various memory improvement methods? *Mrs. Carlson* of Vicore's admitted that the artificial memory-code systems got in the way of natural learning and real comprehension. "The system involved not thinking and reasoning," she said, "but pure and simple memory." *Dr. Ray Hyman,* professor of psychology at the University of Oregon, said of mnemonic systems, "They are not very useful except as parlor stunts (he used to be a magician). They've never been of any real practical help to me. I've found myself better off not using them." Then he related a humorous associational dilemma which is not at all infrequent, "I've got a mental picture of one man I met who had a nose of an odd shape. I visualized it with water running over it. To this day, I can't recall if he is Mr. Brooks, Mr. Rivers or Mr. Trout!"

We know that realistic artwork does indeed illuminate a Scripture text for a child who cannot yet read. Simple associations may afford some memory help, particularly with respect to remembering Bible references. Yet as a whole, we believe that the various memory improvement methods tend to obscure the meaning of the subject being learned, and actually get in the way of natural memorization. Rather than taking time to develop all the involved associations, it is better just to learn the verse by natural concentration and enjoy the subject matter while you are doing it.

Strangely enough, *Mr. Lorayne* finally agreed that the extravagant memory methods were not profitable, when he said, "By using sneaky things in encouraging people to believe they can be mental wizards and getting them to concentrate on these methods, I am forcing them to do what they should do in the first place, so they wouldn't need a memory system."

We come back, therefore, to the simple conclusion that we assimilate the word of God through the well-known mental exercise called *concentration*. You really cannot remember something unless you concentrate on it. In so doing, you try to block everything else out of your mind and set your full attention on the word of the Lord. The mind either concentrates or wanders. Keeping the mind fixed on the sacred text pleases God, who commands us *to lay up His words in our hearts* (Job 22:22). It also honors the Holy Spirit whose mission it is to bring God's word to our remembrance (Jn. 14:26).

Recently, I came across an interesting testimony of a serviceman who wrote me about "the joy of learning the lessons each week." "However," he continued, "I must say that it was difficult at times to learn them. But if I would *concentrate* on what I was doing and followed the suggested plan of memorization, it was much easier than if I went about it half-heartedly. Not only have I added more verses to my memory, but I also use the lessons and explanations for devotions in our church" (*Michael S. Nye*).

We are not attempting to condemn the use of

mnemonics as such, but we are endeavoring to point out that simple concentration is preferable. Consider the blessing of memorizing Romans 15:13: *"Now"*— not last week—but "now"—not tomorrow, but right "now"—"the God of hope" (God never gives up hope concerning a single one of His children) "fill you with all joy and peace in believing..." Things are not *hopeless*, they are *hope-filled*. Continue on with the verse: "that you may abound in hope..." What kind of hope is that? Why, it's like that of "the God of hope." And you are enthralled by this hope "through the power of the Holy Spirit" who dwells in you.

It is wonderful just to think upon the different words and phrases of holy writ and meditate upon them. You are blessed in the very process of assimilating the words and thoughts that the living God has given us. *Einstein* is reported to have said meditatively, "I want to know how God created the world... I want to know His thoughts; the rest are details." Why did not someone tell the intellectual giant in physics that God has revealed His thoughts recorded in a book called "Bible?"

13

Pressures

Is it not the pressures of this life that keep young people and adults from memorizing God's word?

Think about it as we examine some of these "enemies" and see if this may not be the area where your problem lies.

(1) *The pressure of time.* Over and over again people say: "I just don't have the time to do it." There is no denying the fact that we all seem to be pushed with more things to do than we have time. But as you honestly reflect upon this dilemma, is it not generally true that we all manage to find time somehow for those things that we really desire to do? We take care of those things that seem to matter most. In the final analysis it is a matter of setting up the right priorities. How many days do we rush out to meet the world having spent 50 minutes bathing, perfuming, and arranging the outer person and only 10 on any aspect of feeding on God's word, nourishing the inner self. Time is indeed very precious, and we are instructed to be "redeeming the time" because the days are evil (Eph. 5:16,17), and they are also very brief.

Often the plea of insufficient time is advanced by

pastors and other busy Christian workers. It is primarily to all of us who engage in some form of the Lord's work that *Dr. Webb Garrison* directed his poignant remarks some years ago: "Dare I say it?" he began, "I wonder whether perhaps more of the Lord's work would be done if Christian leaders (paid and volunteer) would divert half an hour a day away from activities that produce results on the statistical tables and zealously spend it memorizing and repeating Scripture." Indeed, "the husbandman that laboreth must be first partaker of the fruits" (2 Tim. 2:6).

Even fifteen minutes a day spent thoughtfully in concentrating on the word would make a big difference. Do you think you could afford that much time on a regular basis?

(2) *The pressure of earning a living*: The job, the home chores, the school requirements and all other "cares of this life" seem always to assert themselves convincingly against spiritual pursuits. We feel naturally obligated to place them first.

There is no question but that we do have to take care of these legitimate responsibilities, but here we must give due attention to the words of our Lord— "Take no thought for your life," He said, "what you shall eat, or what you shall drink; nor yet for your body, what you shall put on. Is not the life more than meat and the body than raiment? . . . (For after all these things do the Gentiles seek): for your heavenly Father knoweth that you have need of all these things." And here comes the sound word of instruction to all of us. Ponder it—"but seek ye first the kingdom of God and His righteousness," our Lord declared, "and all these things shall be added unto you" (Matt. 6:25, 32, 33).

How does that sound? Do you think that perhaps you should give priority time to assimilating the word of God?

Earning a living is certainly necessary, but God would also have us know "that man doth not live by bread only, but by every word that proceedeth out of the mouth of the Lord doth man live" (Deut. 8:3). It is very easy in our fast-moving society these days to feast the body and to famish the soul. We lose appetite for the word, spiritual anemia sets in, and although we may have Bibles on every hand, we become overtaken by the "famine . . . of hearing the words of the Lord" (Amos 8:11).

(3) *The pressure of feeling incapable*: So often we listen to the excuse sounded, "I just cannot memorize." Most frequently this is spoken by adults.

It is an interesting phenomenon that although children do not generally understand the Scriptures as well, and do not possess the same measure of appreciation for the word, yet they memorize faster and retain longer than the average adult. One reason undoubtedly is because they are largely free from the "cares of this life."

Isaac Watts, the great hymn writer, made some interesting observations many years ago. He said, "In old age, men have a very feeble remembrance of things that were done of late, that is, the same day or week or year; the brain has grown so hard, that the present images or strokes make little or no impression, and thereby they immediately vanish . . ." He states further that as we get older, the brain shrinks and hardens from lack of use, and that the best therapy for the brain is to exercise it in memorizing, and, of course, the best thing to memorize is Scripture.

Unquestionably there are a few people around who may find it quite impossible to memorize, although even such should not give up. But by and large we can all memorize God's word if we definitely desire to do it. First ask the Lord to help you. He will indeed help because He has instructed us to do it: "Therefore shall you lay up these my words in your heart and in your soul" (Deut. 11:18). He commands us to do it, and He most certainly will grant His enabling grace in accomplishing it. We are all aware of the fact that "without Him we can do nothing" (Jn. 15:5), but as we draw closer to our Lord and allow His strength and wisdom to become our portion, we will be amazed at His enabling power, and we shall confidently exclaim with the Apostle, "I can do all things through Christ which strengtheneth me" (Phil. 4:13).

(4) *The pressure that comes* as a result of not being able to retain and recall all the verses that have been memorized.

First, let us be reminded that the only way anybody can possibly retain a large number of the verses memorized is by constant use of those Scriptures and by an intelligent review of them in a systematic way. Reciting them out loud to someone at home, at school or at work helps tremendously to seal them in your mind. Furthermore, you must not become too concerned if you find yourself unable to recall all of them.

Second—and this is very important—we must not allow ourselves to think that *all* of the verses memorized are forgotten. This simply is not true. We never quite forget all that we have diligently memorized.

Test yourself. Is it not true that when you hear a speaker using one of those Scriptures you thought had completely eluded you, that you recognize it at least in part? Furthermore, the message of the speaker becomes much more meaningful to you. The same is true in your Bible reading. When you come across a verse you have memorized, your mind reacts with enthusiasm and greater interest. The verses memorized become "landmarks" in your Bible reading.

In addition, you must not forget that if you give

attention to memorizing God's word, the Holy Spirit will bring it to your remembrance in that special time of need (Jn. 14:26), and He will bless your heart with truths which you were possibly not in the habit of recalling. Remember this fact, please. On the other hand, He cannot bring to your remembrance Scripture if you have made no effort to store them in your mind and heart.

But supposing that you did forget every verse that you have memorized, there is still immense value because of the blessing you received in the very process of committing God's word to memory.

I read about the man who complained to his pastor that he was much discouraged in memorizing the Scriptures because he could not fasten anything in his memory that would remain. The wise, elderly pastor had him take a pitcher and fill it with water. When he had done so, the pastor bade him to empty it completely and wipe it clean with a cloth. "Now," said the pastor, "though there be nothing of the water remaining in it, yet the pitcher is cleaner than it was before. So, though your memory may seemingly retain nothing of the word you memorized, yet your heart is cleaner because the word went through it."

In my early years, a lady came to me after a service in East Texas, and said, "I simply can't remember anything, because my mind is like a sieve; the word just runs through it." Maybe I was not very polite, but I replied, "Keep memorizing the word, sister; it will keep your mind clean while it's running through."

(5) *Satanic resistance*: And apart from all this, we must always remember that Satan hates the word of God, and he will move heaven and earth to keep you from assimilating it. This is probably Satan's best kept secret. He is very busy in this area and will do everything in his power to pressure you with the cares of

this life and with various deceptions in order to hinder you from laying up God's word in your mind.

This is a spiritual battle. Resist Satan and his attempts to rush you and to crowd you with the responsibilities of this life and the pleasures of this life. He never takes a vacation, so be on the alert and by the grace of God resist his subtle manipulations of your life. God is sovereign. He knows what you need. He loves you most dearly. He cares for you. He desires that you should be joy-filled and fruitful in your Christian life and service. Believe Him and ask Him to help you enjoy the precious word of life. Don't let the busyness of this life keep you from receiving the nourishment and blessedness that God has for you in His word. "Where the word of a king is, there is power" (Ecc. 8:4). As the word of the King of kings is in the heart, there is power against sin, there is power against anxiety, there is power against the manifold trials that come our way. Satan knows that he will be defeated in your life in proportion to the way you allow the word of God to "dwell richly" in your heart (Col. 3:16).

Another powerful enemy in this field is the world system which is largely under the control of Satan. The great area of entertainment has no place for the word of God and its teachings. In the field of education your ignorance of what God says in His word is most generously forgiven. Your peers in school do not generally admire your devotion to God and your eagerness to know His word. Some of your friends will consider you strange, and maybe even weird, because you carry a Bible memory book in your pocket.

But be of good cheer, the word of God is "forever settled in heaven" (Ps. 119:89), and shall never pass away (Matt. 24:35).

"Be strong in the Lord and in the power of His

might" (Eph. 6:10), and keep the sword of the Spirit burnished and ready.

Relaxing

A good many years ago, at the conclusion of a service in Memphis, Tennessee, a man came to talk with me about his frustrations in trying to memorize Scripture. "I believe God wants me to memorize His word," he said, "and I see the need of it in my life, but I just cannot do it; if I continue in this way, I'm afraid I'll have a nervous breakdown." As the dear brother unburdened his problem to me, he became progressively more agitated at the very thought of his predicament. Then he stopped abruptly and turned to me with this question, "Do you have any suggestions which might help me?"

"Yes indeed," I replied, "relax, enjoy it ... you have nothing better to do."

A number of years ago, the Lord showed me very clearly that being occupied with Him over the word was the most important part of my life. We are so much in the habit of thinking that the things in this life which so strongly assert themselves must have immediate attention or else all of life will collapse. The immediateness of the stuff and things around us becomes very disconcerting and distracting. But it occurred to me that I actually did not have to be concerned about how long it took to memorize a certain passage of Scripture because I really did not have anything more important or more urgent to do. This has helped me all along the way, and I have passed the observation on to many.

It really does not matter how long it takes to memorize a passage. Just relax and relish the sweetness of the word as you joyfully try to place the very words of God into the memory chambers of your mind. Think about the meaning of it! Consider each word, each phrase, each sentence. Say it out loud; say it to yourself or to others; say it with expression and with personal conviction. This is indeed the word of God and you are placing great significance on it, and you are putting it into the long-term memory area of your mind.

And so with all the Scripture available in our long-term memory, we may learn to resist pressures to be about other duties and to relax and revel in the wealth of God's word.

I often think of how relaxed and relaxing the word of God really is.

Meditate for just a few minutes on Psalm 63.

The psalmist *awakens*, and at once thirsts for a renewed sense of the Lord's presence (1-2): "O God, thou art my God; early will I seek Thee; my soul thirsteth for Thee, my flesh longeth for Thee in a dry and thirsty land, where no water is; to see Thy power and Thy glory, so as I have seen Thee in the Sanctuary." It is quite obvious that this man is occupied—mind, soul and spirit—with the presence of the Lord and not with the schedule that lies ahead of him for that day.

In the next verses (3-5), there is an expression of grateful praise: "Because Thy lovingkindness is better than life, my lips shall praise Thee. Thus will I bless Thee while I live: I will lift up my hands in Thy name. My soul shall be satisfied as with marrow and fatness; and my mouth shall praise Thee with joyful lips."

The thought of the Lord's presence and His lovingkindness is regarded as "better than life." The day seems to have passed quickly as the pilgrim was occupied with the Lord; all through the day his soul followed hard after Him (vs. 8).

In the evening, he recalls God's mercies (6-8): "When I remember Thee upon my bed, and meditate on Thee in the night watches. Because Thou hast been my help, therefore in the shadow of Thy wings will I rejoice. My soul followeth hard after Thee; Thy right hand upholdeth me." He rejoices in the Lord's protecting and sustaining care.

14

Forgetting

Many sincere people engaged in memorizing Scripture are often troubled by the fact that they cannot remember all that they have memorized.

But forgetting is not all bad. Indeed it is a great help in memorizing Scripture to be able to forget some things. A good "forgetterie" becomes a valuable asset in remembering what is desirable. A well trained memory is one that permits you to forget everything that isn't worth remembering.

What then is the secret of forgetting?

Do not repeat, reread or rethink unimportant material which you have heard or read. By determining not to give it a second chance in your memory, it will lose out in the remembering process.

This is vital. Valueless information, trivia and pointless facts which pour into the brain through the senses continually are a great hindrance to remembering things that are desirable. All this worthless clutter reduces the power of your memory and creates an interference with the retention of the things that you want to remember.

While we are often annoyed by not being able to

remember certain things, we are actually more troubled and distracted by the things we are not able to
forget. *Dr. William Lyon Phelps*, a true believer in God's
word, who was the distinguished head of the English
literature department at Yale University in the early
part of this century, tells about a painful incident in
Joseph Conrad's novel *Almayer's Folly*. It is where the
daughter tells her father she is going away forever; that
he will never see her face again. She leaves the house,
walks through the sand to the edge of the water, takes
the boat and disappears from view. Then the anguished father, moving on his hands and knees, carefully
obliterates every trace of his daughter's footsteps from
the sand on the ground; but he cannot take her feet out
of his heart.

Although memory is generally a source of joy and
delight, it may also be a cause of deep agony.

A full sanctification of the memory requires that
we forget certain things:

(1) *It would be a blessed thing if we could forget the
remembrance of our injuries.* The sense of personal
injury by others is aggravated by remembrance:
"Wounded in the house of my friends" (Zech. 13:6)
and "mine own familiar friend, in whom I trusted,
which did eat of my bread, hath lifted up his heel
against me" (Ps. 41:9). This is a battle that, by the grace
of God, we must win, or it will consume our self-
control, our gentleness, our meekness, and fill the
chambers of our memory with bitterness and gloom.
To forgive is important, but as the poet, *Robert Brown-
ing*, admonished, "Good to forgive; best to forget."

> Forget the praise that falls on you,
> The moment you have won it.
> Forget the slander that you hear,
> Before you can repeat it;
> Forget each slight, each spite, each sneer,
> Wherever you may meet it."

(2) *We must forget our forgotten sins.* There is the sin of yesterday which we have confessed, and which the gracious Lord has forgiven, and yet we turn to it again and again with heaviness of heart. We go back and dig it up again when the Lord Himself has buried it, and over its grave He has planted the lilies of peace. And if we should ever find ourselves in those fields of defeat, we ought to pluck and bring back with us a lily of peace, and testify to the glory of God that where sin abounded "grace doth much more abound." There ought to be no room in our memories for the heaviness and anguish of sin which has been completely forgiven and *forgotten* by God, who declares, "I will remember their sin no more" (Jer. 31:34).

Is not that enough positive instruction, dear friends, for us to do likewise?

(3) *It would be profitable for us also if we did not retain in our memory past victories and attainments.* It is really true that some men's chains are forged from their achievements. We linger over past days and gloat over our successes. When we thus sit down and begin to contemplate our triumphs, progress and fruitfulness will decline. We must give earnest heed to the Apostle's strong determination to forget "those things which are behind ... and press toward the mark for the prize of the high calling of God in Christ Jesus" (Phil. 3:13-14). Much ground yet remains to be possessed.

The grace of God is the only provision for the protection of the memory. "Let this mind be in you which was also in Christ Jesus," who yielded His rights (Phil. 2:5-8), who reviled not again, who threatened not, "but committed Himself to Him that judgeth righteously" (1 Pet. 2:23). "Let this mind be in you," the Apostle insists. We need a sanctified memory—God help us!

It is a matter of debate in the field of psychology whether or not the brain retains everything for all time, but is it not wonderful to realize that God does indeed forget our sins: "I, even I, am He that blotteth out thy transgressions for mine own sake, and will not remember thy sins" (Isa. 43:25). Therefore, as we endeavor to memorize His word, let us pray as did the saint of old, "Lord, help us to *remember* what we ought not to forget, and to *forget* what we ought not to remember."

When these inward hindrances are cleared from the mind, we will much better be able to concentrate on the blessed word of God.

15

Meditating

Meditation is a process of unhurried thought and reflection upon the meaning of the word. Memorizing Scripture makes meditation possible day and night. In turn, meditation facilitates a better understanding and sinks the roots of God's precepts more deeply into memory's recesses.

Memorizing Scripture without the valuable exercise of meditation is like eating food without the process of digestion.

"Scriptures are not meant to be swallowed whole,
They are meant for deep meditation."

Prayerful, devout reflection upon the word infuses every area of life with the solid nutriment of the word. Such meditation causes the whole being to become immersed in the Scriptures, the mind to become saturated with holy thoughts, the heart to be motivated with holy affections and the memory to be filled with holy associations. And we may be very certain that every time the recollection of the blessed word crosses our minds, it is the Holy Spirit's fulfillment of our Lord's promise that "He shall teach you all things, and

bring all things to your remembrance, whatsoever I
have said unto you" (Jn. 14:26).

> Scriptures are stored in our memories
> And the Spirit makes application;
> In times of need, He helps us recall them
> And see their proper relation.
> —Marie Harrington

The "blessed man" in Psalm 1 is able to withstand
the influence of the "ungodly," the "sinners" and the
"scornful" because "his delight is in the law of the
Lord, and in His law doth he meditate day and night."

God is able to reveal to us deeper meanings as we
spend time pondering over His word. Several years
ago, a friend from West Virginia was thrilled in making
this discovery: "How great a blessing your memory
plan has been to me," she said, "I never cease to be
amazed at how often the topic and verses seem to be
exactly what I needed that very week! It's also amazing
how as you go over the words, deeper meanings and
insights just sort of unfold. I don't retain the verses as
well as I would like, but it would be worth taking the
course just for the blessing it gives as the verses are
meditated on, even if I couldn't remember any of them
a year later" (*Mrs. R. G. Kelso*).

The Testimony of George Mueller

George Mueller discovered after a good many
years of serving the Lord, that instead of beginning his
day with prayer, it was much more profitable "to begin
to meditate on the word of God, searching as it were
into every verse to get the blessing out of it . . . in order
to obtain food for my own soul . . . so that, though I did
not as it were, give myself to prayer, but to meditation,
yet it turned almost immediately more or less into
prayer . . . food for my soul is the object of my medita-

ting. The result of this is that there is always a good deal of confession, thanksgiving, supplication, or intercession mingled with my meditation."

Keep In Memory

After concentrating on the word in memorizing, take time to recollect and to repeat the things that have been learned. Think upon them. Meditate. Share them with others. At all cost, do not allow the rich treasures of God's word to be washed away from your memory by a torrent of other activities, nor let them become crowded out by the demands of other affairs. Satan is always eager to reduce or nullify the blessing of the word. He wants to "snatch" it away from your memory.

Is not this the meaning of that "good ground," where "in an honest and good heart, having heard the Word," they "keep it" (Lu. 8:15)? The word for "keep" is *katecho* and specifically, it means "to keep in memory," as it is translated in 1 Corinthians 15:2.

Satan knows how potent God's word is and how it produces spiritual results when allowed to take root in the good soil of the mind and heart. He resorts to many expedients in an effort to remove God's word from the mind. He will remind us about the "cares of this life"; he will get us all worked up over the "deceitfulness of riches" and "the pleasures of this life." In this parable, our Lord sought to emphasize how exceedingly necessary it is for the believer *to keep the word in memory*, to think upon it, to meditate on it, to hold it fast, and allow it to "bring forth fruit with patience" (Lu. 8:15).

Amy Carmichael (1867-1951) penned four lines which abound with instruction on meditation:

"Think through me thoughts of God,
My Father quiet me,

> Till in Thy holy presence hushed,
> I think Thy thoughts with Thee."

Isn't it wonderful to be able to think God's thoughts? When we meditate and think upon the words from God, we may be sure that we are thinking God's thoughts with Him.

I have been profoundly blessed for months in recollecting these precious four lines. I sing them to the melody of "Breathe on me breath of God." I go on with other words:

> Work through me works of God,
> My Father quiet me,
> Till in Thy holy presence hushed,
> I work Thy works with Thee.

> Sing through me songs of God,
> My Father quiet me,
> Till in Thy holy presence hushed,
> I sing Thy songs with Thee.

Everybody, more or less, meditates, but not everybody meditates on the Scriptures. Meditation, apart from the word, quickly degenerates at best into profitless daydreaming, or it becomes a time of dwelling upon our losses, our disappointments and all the other unhallowed recollections.

David rose to the heights of heavenly contemplation when he exclaimed, "Oh how love I Thy law! it is my meditation all the day . . ." He was aware of how God ministered to him through the word. It made him "wiser" and enabled him to have "more understanding." It kept him from "every evil way," and helped him to discern the "false teachings." Prolonged meditation on God's own words only increased his appetite for more of it: "How sweet are Thy words unto my taste! Yea, sweeter than honey to my mouth" (Ps. 119: 97-104).

Recalling the Word in Time of Need

From time to time we all experience sorrow, anguish and a wide variety of trials, and never do they seem to be more acute than in the night seasons when sleep is slow in coming and we are besieged with useless recollections and fearful speculations. We struggle against the powers of darkness which seem to close in on us with cruel threatenings.

Then the "small rain" of the word (Deut. 32:2) begins to fall gently as we meditate. God renews our dejected spirit and feeds us those satisfying morsels of contentment through His word. He speaks to us in His inspired word, and bright hope shines amidst the thick darkness! Therefore, let us "remember" Him and "meditate" on Him "in the night watches" (Ps. 63:6).

But is it not true that we can only recall and meditate in this way on what we already know? Thanks be unto God that we have that solid and abiding word of the Lord in our memory bank.

The Example of Jeremiah

Consider the prophet Jeremiah as he tells of his deep despair in Lamentations chapter 3. Though the adversities and the ensuing darkness came to him from his enemies, he regarded his afflictions as coming from the Lord Himself: "He has led me, and brought me into darkness... He has set me in dark places... He has hedged me about... He has made my chain heavy ... He shuts out my prayer ... He has pulled me in pieces; He has made me desolate ... He has filled me with bitterness." Then the anguished, tormented prophet turns to God directly and cries out, "Thou hast removed my soul far off from peace," and brooding over his desperate condition he concludes his lament of hopelessness, "My strength and my hope is perished from the Lord" (Lam. 3:6-18).

It is hard to imagine any state of heart and mind that is more hopeless.

But wait a minute! Is not this the prophet who had the word of the Lord so clearly revealed to him? Is not this the man who proclaimed it so vigorously during those dark days when the captivity of Judah was approaching? Was not this the one who testified concerning the blessing of having the word, saying as he did, "Thy words were found and I did eat them, and Thy word was unto me the joy and rejoicing of my heart" (Jer. 15:16)?

Yes indeed, this is the man!

But now read on in Lamentations chapter 3, and notice the remarkable change that suddenly comes upon the prophet as he remembers God's word.

Notice what he is now saying, "This I recall to my mind, therefore have I hope" (Lam. 3:21).

Jeremiah is no longer in a state of utter despair. He now has hope in the Lord. He recalls the word of God and this brings wonderful hope and peace. Notice the substance of what he *recalls*, "It is of the Lord's mercies that we are not consumed, because His compassions fail not. They are new every morning." And we can almost hear him raising his voice as he joyfully exclaims, "Great is Thy faithfulness . . . The Lord is my portion, says my soul; therefore will I hope in Him."

Is it not truly wonderful how our whole outlook changes when we can "recall" and meditate upon some appropriate portion of the word of the Lord?

You Must Take Time

This is all well and good, some of you are probably saying, but I can hardly find time to memorize the Scriptures, much less taking time for meditation! But any Bible reading or memorization that is not followed by meditation is like rain on a sieve.

Dear friend—whoever you are—you simply must take time to meditate on God's word, or you will most certainly be drying up!

It is not the splash of diving into the sea, but actually staying there a while that results in the gathering of the goodly pearls!

Consider the example of the Apostle Paul. He was a very, very busy pioneering missionary and preacher! Agreed? Well, we find in Acts 20:13-14 that his missionary companions sailed from Troas to Assos, but Paul "minding himself to go on foot" that ten or fifteen miles. Why did he do this? Was he tired of his fellow-laborers? Not likely. It appears that Paul felt the great need of being alone with the Lord and he planned that solitary walk for the specific purpose of prayer, meditation and quiet communion with the Lord.

Of all people, the Lord's servants must at all cost somehow find time to assimilate God's word, to meditate on it day and night and to commune alone with the Lord, or else they will become mere religious propagandists.

The time of meditation is not to be for vague imaginings, but for living, practical blessing, whether in the form of guidance, counsel, comfort, warning or rebuke.

As you meditate on the word of God, there will continually accrue to your spiritual account–uplifting, enriching benefits, carrying your life to ever higher plateaus of usefulness and blessing.

Summary
Consider thoughtfully the summarization of what we have been trying to say in this chapter:

1) It is by *meditation* that we sink the word more deeply into our memory. It becomes one of the most effective forms of review.

2) It is through *meditation* that we come to understand the Scripture better and draw out the deep truths which before seemed to be concealed.

3) It is by *meditation* that we draw out various inferences and establish in our minds spiritual principles relating to Bible knowledge.

4) It is by *meditation* upon the word that we are enabled to evaluate what we read and hear, and by the illumination of the Holy Spirit, distinguish between truth and error.

5) *Meditation* in the word is the surest way of meeting with the Lord in sweet communion.

6) *Meditation* upon the word soon turns to communion with the Lord, and then to fervent prayer where we use the inspired promises and praises in our intercessions and our thanksgivings.

7) At other times, Scriptures which have been brought together in the mind through memorization and *meditation*, instead of remaining scattered, as it were, they have a way of forming an unexpected cohesion and producing new and fresh insights into the wonderful word of God.

In our day of much activity and much going to and fro, *meditation* seems to have become a lost art. We do not strive to improve the capacity for sustained thought on a given subject, nor are we eager to engage in a prolonged, quiet consideration of the word of truth. This represents an area of great spiritual need. Having memorized God's word, let us go a step further and reap the wonderful benefits which God has for those who will take time to "delight" in His statutes and to "meditate" in His precepts (Ps. 119:15-16).

Casual reading of the Bible is like a bee skimming over the surface of a flower, but memorizing the Scripture is where the bee penetrates into the depths of the blossom to secure the nectar. Then the meditation upon the word is like the bee taking the nectar home and making it into honey for its own use and for the benefit of others.

The Master walks in His garden,
Searching with watchful air
For traces of blight or blemish
On the objects of His care.
Here is a branch that wildly
Clambers over the wall;
Its many leaves are broad and green,
But its fruit is scattered and small.

Tenderly now, but firmly,
The Master with careful touch
Trims off the useless tendrils—
Enough, but not too much.
Tenderly now and lovingly,
Breathing low words of cheer:
"Take courage, branch, for thou art Mine,
Thou wilt bear more fruit next year."

If I, the branch, wild growing,
Have need of the pruning-knife,
Can I not trust the Master
With all things, yea, with life?
Can I not trust His tender care
O'er leaf and twig and shoot,
Hoping at last, in harvest-time,
That I shall bring forth fruit?

—Mrs. C. Scoville

16

Appropriating

We memorize Scripture with a definite purpose in mind. It is not just for the sake of knowing a certain number of verses but in order to be able to use them and apply them in real life. This also becomes one of the best forms of remembering and reviewing the verses.

James, who emphasized the practical side of the Christian life, wrote, "But be ye doers of the word, and not hearers only, deceiving your own selves" (1:22). The real test of Scriptures "learned" lies not in the ability to recite them word for word, but in the understanding and the application of the truth in daily living. The word of God works effectually in a life when it is received, believed and appropriated as the very word of God (1 Thess. 2:13).

Memorizing Scripture must always be with the view of *obedience* and *submission* to God. "This book of the Law shall not depart out of thy mouth; but thou shalt meditate therein day and night, that thou mayest observe to do according to all that is written therein..." (Josh. 1:8). The internal movement of the soul is definitely affected and motivated by meditation on the word, as is expressed by the psalmist, "I thought on my ways, and turned my feet unto Thy testimonies. I made haste, and delayed not to keep Thy command-ments" (119:59-60).

Appropriating the Word

Many of us have been strengthened by the earnest testimony of *Joni Eareckson Tada*: She said in her book which she wrote by holding the pen in her mouth, "I memorized Scripture portions that had great meaning to me. Understanding these messages that spoke to me to better trust God with my will as well as my life. Even when distressing or despondent times came along, I could depend on the fact that 'He knew what He was doing,' as daddy frequently said. Through memorizing God's promises, I learned that the Lord would take me out of training in this school of suffering —but in His own good time."

There are many among the Lord's people who have been greatly helped by the courageous life and testimony of *Eugene L. Clark, Nebraska*. I had the joy of meeting him. Although crippled with arthritis and his body racked with pain, he never complained but con-tinued with his service for the Lord in writing music for *Back to the Bible Broadcast*.

He wrote as follows: "Memorizing the Scripture under your plan during the past five years has been an immeasurable blessing. One reason that it cannot be measured is that by systematically memorizing the word on a regular basis, we tend to absorb it into our lives and it becomes part of us. I have found your plan challenging and workable. The attractive way in which the verses are presented and the incentives along the way have been extremely helpful and useful.

"About ten years ago, I lost my eyesight and became bedfast with arthritis. Carrying on a useful ministry and raising a family of three children under these challenging conditions have led my wife, Ferne, and me to trust the Lord for many things, and to re-evaluate our lives in the light of His word.

"We are convinced that the effectiveness of a life or a ministry is directly in proportion to its closeness to God's word. The Lord instructed Joshua to meditate in His word day and night and then he would have good success. This principle in Joshua chapter 1 was the experience of the Psalmist in Psalm 1, and was reiterated by Jesus in His illustration of the vine and the branches in John chapter 15."

Often as Christians we pass through difficult circumstances and become hard pressed because we fail to draw upon the promises of God which we have memorized. You may remember the incident in *Pilrim's Progress* when *Christian* and *Hopeful* were in the dungeon of *Giant Despair*, and were advised by the Giant to commit suicide. Here is Bunyan's account of what took place:

"At this they trembled greatly, and I think that Christian fell into a swoon; but coming a little to himself again, they renewed their discourse about the Giant's counsel; and whether they had best to take it or no. Now Christian again seemed to be for doing it, but Hopeful made his second reply as follows: 'My Brother,' said he, 'rememberest thou not how valiant thou hast been heretofore. *Apollyon* could not crush thee, nor could all that thou didst hear or see or feel in the Valley of the Shadow of Death . . .'

"Well, on Saturday about midnight they began to pray, and continued in prayer till almost break of day. Now a little before it was day, good Christian broke out in his passionate speech, 'What a fool,' said he, 'am I to lie in a stinking dungeon, when I may as well be at liberty! I have a Key in my bosom, called *Promise*, that will, I am persuaded, open any lock in Doubting Castle.' Then said Hopeful, 'That's good news; good brother pluck it out of thy bosom and try.' "

The "Key" worked and they went on their way rejoicing.

We are all engaged in a spiritual warfare—and our antagonists are not just flesh and blood, but they are subtle, strong and savage "principalities... powers... rulers of the darkness of this age . . . spiritual wickedness in high places" (Eph. 6:6-12). We need to discover as much as possible where our battleground lies and the nature of our spiritual struggle so that we may the more effectively appropriate the God-given armor in resisting the fiery darts and the pernicious onslaught of the devil. We would be strongly tempted to faint and give up at once if we did not remember the pertinent word from God which says, "Greater is He that is in you than he that is in the world" (1 Jn. 4:4).

"Many times I have used the verses learned in your plan," writes *Don Sweaton*, Florida, "to resist the temptations of the devil."

God's word is the means of victory and blessing in every situation. When memorized it becomes instantly accessible in every time of need.

In Resisting Temptations

A variety of temptations will come. They come always and they come to each one of us—young and older.

Temptation originates within the heart of the sinner himself. It is useless for us to blame God, or to say, "the devil made me do it." A person sins when he is "enticed" by the bait, and "drawn away" by the hook of "his own lust." That lust includes the appetites of the body and the evil dispositions of the mind, including pride, malice, envy, love of ease and others.

The attacks of Satan are strong and savage, as he roams about seeking whom he may deceive and devour. His strategies for tripping up the child of God are loaded with subtle allurements. His schemes are long-range, vicious and intent upon thwarting God's purposes in our lives, if possible.

The enemy approaches in the heavy garb of carnality,—"the lust of the flesh"; in the next round he assumes the lighter robe of covetousness,—"the lust of the eyes"; and then, almost resembling the angel of light, he shows up in the delicate attire of vanity,— "the pride of life"! In all the guises, however, it is the same foe, the same devil.

"Wretched man that I am," we cry with the Apostle Paul. What shall we do? From James we hear the command, "Resist the devil, and he will flee from you" (4:7). But the enemy is not easily frightened; he is not easily repulsed; therefore, be vigilant and "resist him steadfast in the faith . . ." and do not forget that "the God of all grace" is ever with you to "stablish, strengthen, settle you" (1 Pet. 5:8-10).

Quickly pick up the God-ordained weapons. For your defense "take" the helmet of salvation, the shield of faith and the breastplate of righteousness (Eph. 6: 14-17). The word "take" means to receive as from the hand of God.

Go on the offensive by taking "the sword of the Spirit which is the word of God." The "word of God" here means "a specific utterance of God," a particular saying. We have for our warfare the very same sword which our Lord used when under heavy attack by Satan (Matt. 4). Thank God that we have committed to memory these *definite, divine utterances of God* so that they are ready for use at that unexpected moment of need. Like a flash, we pull the sharp, two-edged sword from the sheath (memory) and strike the enemy of our souls.

The Bible that is gathering dust,
  A weapon that is showing rust,
Will not suffice to keep us pure,
  Temptation's power to endure,
If we would make the foe depart,
  God's word must be within the heart.
By these words alone the foe is smitten,
  In this our hope: "It is written."

-Tom Welsch

Temptations are sure to knock on our door, but we do not have to invite them in. Instead, receive as from the hand of God ("take") that most appropriate divine "utterance" which you have so neatly filed away in your memory; and suddenly that sword, "wrought and edged by the Holy One Himself" (Moule), will be striking, and you will know that you have "power . . . over all the power of the enemy" (Lu. 10:19).

When you are being enticed in the secrets of your heart, recite a Scripture out loud, and praise the Lord.

God gives the word. We receive it; we assimilate it; we meditate on it; we appropriate it in that hour of sore temptation. "Take fast hold of instruction; let her not go: keep her; for she is thy life" (Prov. 4:13).

The discussion above is how that truth in 1 Corinthians 10:13 works out in real life battles: "There hath no temptation taken you but such as is common to man: but God is faithful, who will not suffer you to be tempted above that ye are able; but will with the temptation also make a way to escape, that ye may be able to bear it."

God Himself provides the way of escape from every temptation through the effectual use of His word (1 Thess. 2:13).

Believest thou this?

In Cleansing From Sin

How can a believer cleanse his way and remain in uninterrupted fellowship with God? Is it by sheer determination never to commit sin? Indeed not! The cleansing comes through the enlightenment and power of the word.

"How shall a young man cleanse his way? By taking heed thereto according to Thy word" (Ps. 119:9). The Holy Spirit takes the quickening word, enlightens the mind and probes the conscience as to God's remedy for sin's defilement. Following the enlightenment and the convicting comes the contrite spirit and the humble confession. And the record says, "If we confess our sins, He" (that is God) "is faithful and just to forgive us our sins, and to cleanse us from all unrighteousness" (1 Jn. 1:9).

A good many years ago, I received a telephone call about midnight from friends in a distant city who were deeply concerned about the gambling habit of their son. He was in the U.S. Army, stationed at that time in the St. Louis area. They desired to send me about a thousand dollars if I would go with their son and pay off the gambling debts. I agreed to do so.

I knew the young man quite well. He had memorized Scripture in our plan for several years and attended our camp. I heard his testimony. He seemed like a true believer. I met with him at the designated place and as we talked, I asked him about his state of fellowship with the Lord. Without saying a word, he began humbly to confess his sin to God. He poured out his heart in deep contrition of spirit before God. You see, the Scriptures he memorized were now actively at work in his life as a child of God. He had something to lay hold of. The word convicted him of his sin and brought the contrition and the confession.

The first thing he said to the men at the house

where they were already gambling was "I am a Christian!"

God gave him the victory through the word.

If the believer willfully persists to live in sin, God will deal with such a person as a father deals with his son. "For whom the Lord loveth He chasteneth, and scourges every son whom He receiveth" (Heb. 12:6).

We all know how very true this is because of God's dealings with us, and because we have observed His ways with others. At such a time, the person being disciplined who has God's word in mind and heart, will respond more quickly and more wholeheartedly. God's word probes and burns. The person will realize that although "no chastening for the present seemeth to be joyous, but grievous: nevertheless afterward it yieldeth the peaceable fruit of righteousness unto them which are exercised thereby" (Heb. 12:11); he will not "despise" the "chastening of the Lord, nor faint" when he is "rebuked" of God (Heb. 12:5).

God's purpose in disciplining His children is always with the view of restoration. He is preparing His children so that they may be compassionate and better able, "in the spirit of meekness," to help restore others who may have been "overtaken in a fault" (Gal. 6:1).

In Times of Severe Trial

The servant of the Lord will often meet with severe trials and discouragements. He will discover in those times of testing that his only sure resource is that precious word of God which he has, perhaps, been recommending so zealously to others.

How blessed it is at such times to be able to draw on God's own words of encouragement like those first spoken to Joshua, "Have not I commanded thee? Be strong and of a good courage; be not afraid, neither be thou dismayed; for the Lord thy God is with thee whithersoever thou goest" (1:9). I recall how some years ago when I was enduring much testing, I arrived at our camp one night, and I found these words, spoken to Joshua, typed out on a card by members of the staff and placed on the dresser in my room. My heart was lifted up, and I began praising the Lord.

Various needs will arise along the way, but God knows that we have need of them, and makes solid provisions: "Thy shoes shall be iron and brass," He told the sons of Asher (Deut. 33:25). What about the aching feet, the feeble knees and the fainting body? What good are the "iron shoes"? Well, beloved, God is aware of that need also, and His promise continues in that same verse, "and as thy days, so shall thy strength be."

Praise the Lord! "Thou hast delivered my soul from death," the Psalmist said, "mine eyes from tears, and my feet from falling. I will walk before the Lord in the land of the living" (Ps. 116:8-9).

The servant of the Lord is renewed as other wonderful promises of God come to mind, and he goes forth "in the strength of the Lord" (Ps. 71:16). He takes fresh courage as he remembers God's promise in Isaiah 55: "My word . . . shall not return unto Me void."

In Seasons of Deep Depression

"When men are cast down, then thou shalt say, There is a lifting up; and God shall save the humble person" (Job 22:29).

There is many a person who has experienced some tragic disappointment, and is enduring unspeakable depression which envelopes him in darkness like a thick cloud, and continues persistently to obscure all hope. He may be too "overwhelmed within his spirit" (Ps. 143:4) to read the word, but as he struggles in that state of depression, he seems to see emblazoned on the wall in front of him, *"Thou wilt keep him in perfect peace whose mind is stayed on Thee!"*

He is startled and mutters to himself, "Why, that's a verse of Scripture that I memorized, and it's found in Isaiah 26:3."

"Perfect peace"—why, that is exactly what he does *not* have. What is the trouble? Why does he not have that "perfect peace"?

Oh, the "mind." Where is it? What is that mind contemplating? What is that mind occupied with hour after hour?

Turn your attention from yourself to the Lord! Think upon the Lord and His great faithfulness. He has never let you down. He has never disappointed you. Let your "mind" be stayed on Him.

Refuse to dwell on those disappointments! Let that mind be steadily stayed upon the Lord, and you will surely hear the parting words of our blessed Lord just as if He were right there in the room with you, "Peace I leave with you, My peace I give unto you."

Oh yes, he needs that peace, but everything has turned against him.

But the Lord continues, "Not as the world giveth give I unto you."

The world affords a measure of quietness when all speak well of you, and when all the circumstances are favorable, but all that sense of well-being blows away when the storm hits.

But the peace of the Lord does not depend upon circumstances; it comes strictly as a result of our relationship to Him. Say those words again, friend: "Peace I leave with you, My peace I give unto you: not as the world giveth, give I unto you."

Say those words out loud! Say them yet again and again until you can relax, and then listen to Him as He completes the rest of that verse: "Let not your heart be troubled, neither let it be afraid" (Jn. 14:27).

"Weeping may endure for a night"—that night may be long—it may last weeks and months—"but joy cometh in the morning" (Ps. 30:5).

"Why art thou cast down, O my soul? and why art thou disquieted with me? hope thou in God: for I shall yet praise Him, who is the health of my countenance" (Ps. 42:11).

"When men are cast down, then thou shalt say, There is a lifting up; and God shall save the humble person" (Job 22:29).

How wonderful, how blessed it is to have that word in your mind and heart! Because, perhaps when you need that word the most, you do not have the desire nor even the strength to reach for the Bible. But when that word is inscribed upon your heart, you can lay hold of it like a flash. You may be pinned under that car or tractor and be unable to turn the pages of the Book, but the Holy Spirit will bring just the right word to your remembrance if you have taken time aforehand to memorize it.

In Seeking Wisdom

Here is another saint who must make an important decision. He desperately needs wisdom. So much depends upon this particular step. He must know the mind of the Lord in it.

Then he *remembers* the words in James on the subject.

"If any of you lack wisdom, let him ask of God."

What will God do?

The Scripture states that God grants true wisdom: "He giveth to all men liberally" (that "all" includes all who ask in faith) "and upbraideth not, and it shall be given him" (Jas. 1:5-6).

God gives wisdom! What kind of wisdom is it? How does God deal with hard-headed people and knotty circumstances?

Then remember another verse you memorized. It is James 3:17, "But the wisdom that is from above is first pure, then peaceable, gentle, and easy to be entreated, full of mercy and good fruits, without partiality and without hypocrisy."

Thank you Lord!

This description of wisdom rings true. It is so definitive, so superlatively complete! The hard-pressed person begins to feel that with such wisdom he can venture out into battle.

Oh, that our minds might be so in tune with the God of all wisdom that in all our dealings with others we may think, react and speak in a quiet and *gentle* manner, words that are "pure"; that in all situations our attitudes would not be adamant, but that we might be "easily entreated"; that we might not push justice until it screams, but be overflowing with "mercy and good fruits," and in every circumstance be free from "partiality and hypocrisy."

In the Days of Sorrow

There are always those around us who are passing through deep sorrow and grief as their loved ones are taken from them. It is true that "they sorrow not as others which have no hope," but, nevertheless, they do sorrow.

We can comfort them only "by the comfort where-with we ourselves are comforted of God" (2 Cor. 1:4). We can pray with them and empathize with them over the word of God. In the end it is the word of God that sustains us when we are called upon to pass through the deep valleys.

Mrs. Louise Brooks, Texas, writes, "The memory

work has blessed my heart these many years. The Scriptures have sustained me during the death of my daughter, and just recently, having been given some very bad news, they kept me from sinking into the depths of despair. Through seasons of sadness and distress, they have enabled me to triumph and rejoice. Through memorizing of the verses, the Holy Spirit can speak to us."

About ten years ago, we received a letter from *Mrs. Lois Coleman* in Louisiana, which, in part, reads as follows: "You see, the Lord called my just grown-up daughter home to Himself. And although I know His ways are perfect, there are times *when praise comes hard.* This little book ("Praising the Lord") set it all in order and helped me to praise the Lord, not the circumstances, through it all."

Sally Ellen Coleman was a radiant Christian. Her mother enrolled her to memorize Scripture in our system when she was only four years of age. She continued memorizing through all the years until she reached the last Collegiate book, when "she had to drop out because of the brain tumor that took her earthly life." Sally Ellen had memorized over 1700 Bible verses.

The word of God prepares a person for life and for death. Sally Ellen wanted to live, but was not afraid of dying. She could say, "It's O.K. Mom," as the silent killer advanced and she and her mother wept together.

"She never complained," her mother said, "she never was afraid." Her earthly body died on Saturday, September 6, 1980, but she is indeed "more alive than ever."

Friends and loved ones surrounding Mrs. Coleman helped and prayed, but it was, as she says, the memorized word which proved "to be just the healing balm I needed."

Perhaps sooner than we think, the trumpet shall sound; the Lord shall return with all the saints who have gone to heaven, and "we shall be caught up together with them in the clouds, to meet the Lord in the air; and so shall we ever be with the Lord."

"Wherefore comfort one another with these words" (1 Thess. 4:13-18).

In Rejoicing Amidst Poverty

Poverty, privations, pain and sickness may be holding you in their threatening grasp.

Think now! Think of that verse you memorized in Psalm 37—"Rest in the Lord"—just let go and let God —"Rest in the Lord and wait patiently for him." *Remember* also the words of our Lord when he said, "Come unto me all ye that labor and are heavy laden, and I will give you rest" (Matt. 11:28).

And as you keep "looking unto Jesus," you may reach that glorious "yet" of Habakkuk: "Although the fig tree shall not blossom, neither shall fruit be in the vines; the labor of the olive shall fail, and the field shall yield no meat; the flock shall be cut off from the fold, and there shall be no herd in the stalls: YET I will rejoice in the Lord, I will joy in the God of my salvation" (3:17-18).

YET . . . Despite all the adversities, and in the midst of them, "yet, I will rejoice in the Lord."

Say it with the prophet, "Yet I will rejoice in the Lord, I will joy in the God of my salvation."

In the Thought Life

All of us, without exception, do battle in the thought life. God's purpose is that the believer would bring "into captivity every thought to the obedience of Christ" (2 Cor. 10:5). God looks less upon the externals of life; He goes straight home to the hearts of men, for "as he thinketh in his heart, so is he" (Prov. 23:7).

In one of his God-breathed epistles, the Apostle Paul lays out a formula for the thought life: "Finally brethren, whatsoever things are true, whatsoever things are honest, whatsoever things are just, whatsoever things are pure, whatsoever things are lovely, whatsoever things are of good report; if there be any virtue and if there be any praise, think on these things" (Phil. 4:8). The Apostle says, "Think on these things"! The emphasis here is not on conduct but on our thoughts. It is not the dirt on our hands, nor the unclean food that defiles a man, but it's the evil thoughts churning in the heart.

God sets about us the whole circle of perfection, and exhorts us to "think on these things." When you awake at night, *think* upon them. In the car, bus, or plane, *think* upon them. In your work, in your school, in your home, let the things of God that are pure and honorable and just and lovely rule all your thoughts, and keep your whole being enthralled with the things that God has for us, and which center in His "altogether lovely" Son, our Lord and Savior Jesus Christ."

Captain James E. Ray, Texas, relates the thrilling account of how the remembered Scriptures kept the men in the Hanoi prison from going mad or becoming animals.

"One night I lay with my ear pressed against the wall to hear 'thump . . . thumpety thump' as somewhere on the wall another P.O.W. tapped out in Morse code: "I will lift up mine eyes unto the hills, from whence cometh my help" (Ps. 121:1). Another time the verse thumped out was: "Man shall not live by bread alone, but by every word that proceedeth out of the mouth of the Lord" (Matt. 4:4).

"The men began to pool the verses they could recall and thus have a 'consensus Bible' among them

. . . Bible verses on paper aren't one iota as useful," Captain Ray said, "as Scriptures burned into your mind where you can draw on them for guidance and comfort."

In the Prayer Life

Scores of friends, both young and older, write to tell how the memorized word stimulates and strengthens their prayer life.

I remember reading about the young lady who was the average kind of church member. She said to her pastor one day, "After all is it not just as well to talk *about* God as to talk *to* God?"

The pastor replied, "How is it about your mother? Is it just as well to talk about her as it is to talk to her?"

"Oh no," she said, "that is different. Mother talks back you know."

She did not seem to know that God talks back to us in His inspired words recorded in the Scriptures.

After we have prayed, we should say, as did the handmaid of old, "Let my Lord the King now speak" (2 Sam. 14:18).

So often we kneel down and go through our prayer requests with considerable earnestness and meaning, but then we quickly get up and rush away from the King's presence as soon as we have had our say, and hardly expect Him to send His answers. Surely, He had something to say to us, but we never waited to hear what His gracious response would be.

How marvelously the two-way conversation of prayer is facilitated when we have God's words already filed away in our memory.

If the Lord delays in answering our prayer, it is, as He had told us in order "that He may be gracious unto us." He reminds us to maintain our implicit trust in Him and then tells us further, "Blessed are all they that wait for Him" (Is. 30:18).

He does not desire His children to become impatient with Him. We do not know exactly how or when He will answer, but He Himself assures us that He will answer all who call (Jer. 33:3) and that it will be very substantial and more than we expected (Jer. 29:11).

And is it not just "super," as the younger set would say, to have those sure words from God neatly locked in our memory. I think that it must be most gratifying to God to realize that we do have them indelibly written in our minds and to hear us articulating them to Him in a spirit of triumphant hope and faith!

Hallelujah! God is good! His word is true, and we are spiritual millionaires!

Those Who Memorize Reap the Blessings

Through the years, thousands of people have written to tell of the blessings and benefits that they have experienced through Bible memorization. Let me cite excerpts from several of them.

Jack Stem, Texas: "For years I resisted memorizing God's word, and I repeatedly said 'no' to those who asked me. Scripture memorizing does not come easily for me, and I didn't want to face the discipline for fifteen weeks of consistent concentration. But I did, and praise the Lord for SMF and for the many blessings that I have received through memorizing God's word. As is often the case in the Christian life, the greatest growth comes as a result of the greatest difficulty . . . Now I delight in filling my mind with the words of my Savior. I wish I had started years ago."

Mrs. Rufina Jenkins, Missouri: "The verses I memorized have served me well in the times of testing and trials that God always allows in the life of His children. I learned through experience the faithfulness and the truthfulness of God's word. An even greater joy came when my husband, Ed, began memorizing at the age of 70. The first year's work awakened his desire to 'know' the Lord in a way he had not had in all his life."

Mrs. Dan Graves, Tennessee: "May I relate one of the most wonderful things that happened? Our seven year old son memorized Elementary Book 1. As he was working in his bedroom on lesson nine,—"The Lord Died For Me"—he came into the living room with tears in his eyes and told me how he wanted to become a Christian right then. He did so."

Mrs. S. A. Franks, California: "I am amazed at the transforming power in these verses as they are committed to memory. They become a part of my being, my *well-being.* The Holy Spirit gives life by the word (2 Cor. 3:6)."

Peter Geisz, Missouri: "I have found that the sweetness of my walk with God seems to coincide almost entirely with the consistency of my Bible memory work."

Dr. & Mrs. David Johnston, Virginia: "Memorized Scripture becomes a part of the person and thus, readily available for God to use to speak to him and *through* him. His word is ready for witness to unbelievers and for comfort and encouragement to those in need. As members of the congregation commit themselves to a program of memorizing Scripture and mature in the Lord, the local church enjoys overflow benefits in willing, joyful servants, exemplary leadership, missionary responsibility and true Christian fellowship in praise and worship. Our appreciation of God—His person and His work—is in direct proportion to our knowledge of and commitment to His word. Memorizing Scripture focuses attention in order to develop a greater appreciation of our wonderful Lord."

Kenneth Gant, Texas: "I memorize Scripture because of the feeling of satisfaction and because it not only helps me, but it also is a great benefit in witnessing to others. It just adds a dimension to our lives that nothing else can."

George Darquea, Illinois: George came from Colombia, South America, and was introduced to our Bible memorizing system by *Jay Lake* at a clothing store in Wheaton, Illinois. George faced many tough problems. One time after reciting the prescribed assignment for that week, he said to Jay: "You know, these Bible verses have *comforted* me so much. I never could have gone on with all the problems I've had if it hadn't been for this experience learning the word of God."

Mrs. Dean Hoodenpyle, Texas: "Hiding God's word in my heart has meant more in my life than my words could ever express. I have gone through times of heartache and life-threatening illness these past several years, but praise God, He has never failed to bring to my memory—at the very time I needed it the most—*just the Scripture* that would see me through. God bless you as you continue."

Jim Woychuk, Missouri (when he was age 13): "I have memorized Bible verses for about ten years, and I was saved as a direct result of memorizing them (2 Tim. 3:15). God has used the verses I have committed to memory in three different areas. First, having memorized verses helps me when I'm praying. Scripture 'lends power to prayer.' Second, knowing portions of God's word is useful to me when I am witnessing to others about the Lord. Third, it helps me at school in day-to-day situations that come up. Having Bible verses in my mind helps me to resist the devil's temptation to sin (Ps. 119:11)."

Mrs. R. L. Fisher, Texas: "For the past five years Amy has been enrolled in Scripture Memory. She has certainly learned a lot of Scripture. She quotes the Scripture to us each week. One night she was reading them to her seven-year-old sister, Gayle. That day Gayle was sad because a handicapped child she knew at school had died. Amy, unknown to us, talked to her about the child and about heaven. She went on to talk to her about being saved. The next morning Gayle came bouncing into the den saying, 'Guess what Amy helped me do last night?' 'What?' we asked. 'She helped me put Jesus in my heart.' "

Remembering and Believing

Appropriation of the word depends so much on two things: remembering and believing.

The children of Israel were reminded of God's miraculous works in delivering them from the bondage in Egypt (Ps. 106:1-11).

Then, somehow their memory faded. Cares and disappointments moved in, and they "forgot His works: they waited not for His counsel" (106:13). The ways of the flesh followed: they lusted, they envied, they promoted idolatry.

Then comes the record of their condition which caused their serious defections: "They believed not His word." Instead of praising Him, they "murmured in their tents, and hearkened not unto the voice of the Lord" (106:24-25).

Spiritual leanness always follows when we neglect God's word and forget His manifold works of grace. May the Lord quicken our minds and help us each day to do our part by "gathering up the forces of memory," and allowing His word to "dwell richly" in our hearts (Col. 3:16), so that we may *remember* all the way in which the Lord our God has led us, protected us and provided for us. In our pilgrim journey, "there hath not failed one word of all His good promise . . ." (1 Kings 8:56).

17

Abiding

"Abide in Me" is our Lord's supreme commandment. To abide in Christ, therefore, becomes the Christian's *greatest responsibility*. Doing it is building *gold*!

This is why memorizing Scripture is so urgent. Having the word of God in the mind and heart is so very essential for abiding in Christ. Meditation upon the word is the means whereby the believer can "abide" in Christ and which opens the way for Christ to "abide" in the believer.

The Lord gave the ten commandments on Mount Sinai, but He gave the *one* great commandment in the upper room guest chamber, and emphasized it by a ten-fold repetition of the word "abide" within seven verses (Jn. 15:4-10).

"Abide in Me" is what Christ is saying to every child of God every moment of every hour of every day. If there is to be "fruit," He must work through us, from beginning to end, just as the vine works through the branches.

To *abide* in Christ means to enjoy Him, to delight in Him, to love Him and to worship Him. To *abide* in Christ means to trust Him in every situation, to keep the mind and heart ever open to Him, and to have His word abiding within. It involves, also, walking in the light as He is in the light, and having a sincere desire to be done with sin and a joyful readiness to do His will.

"Abide in Me, and I in you. As the branch cannot bear fruit of itself, except it abide in the vine; no more can ye, except ye abide in Me. I am the vine, ye are the branches: he that abideth in Me, and I in him, the same bringeth forth much fruit: for without Me ye can do nothing" (Jn. 15:4-5).

This is an *awakening* truth! *J. Hudson Taylor's* life took on new meaning when he began "living in John Fifteen." He said, "As I thought of the vine and the branches, what light the blessed Spirit poured directly into my soul. Oh the joy of seeing this truth."

The point of comparison in this Scripture between the vine and Christ is the organic union by means of which the life of the vine-stock becomes the life of the branches. As the sap which rises into the branches is that which comes from the vine, so the life in the believers will be that which will flow from the risen, living Lord.

Abide

The word "abide" is peculiar to the Apostle John. It acquires a new and more forceful meaning in his writings. He uses the word in its original form—*meno* in Greek—forty one times in the Gospel and twenty six times in his epistles. In the King James translation it is rendered also in other words including "dwell," "remain," "continue," "endure." In every instance it could have been translated "abide."

Abiding in Christ represents not only the greatest responsibility of every child of God, but it is an absolute essential; for "without Me," the Lord said, "ye can do nothing" (Jn. 15:5). The command to "abide" in Christ is in essence His gracious plea to let Him abide in the believer, who is the expression of His life and witness in this world.

David Livingstone (1813-1873) discovered Africa and he also discovered the Africans. He walked from Cape Town to Victoria Falls: he went west to the Atlantic and east to the Indian Ocean, preaching the gospel and evangelizing. His heart lies buried in that giant continent while his body is entombed in Westminster Abbey.

Andrew Murray (1828-1917) spent his life in that same land teaching the believers how to "abide" in Christ. Some two hundred fifty publications came from his pen, but the one which continues teaching God's people most widely in numerous translations is the book, "Abide in Christ."

Abide in Me, and I in you

"Abide in Me, and I in you" is not an exhortation to remain in *union* with Christ; that occurs when a person is regenerated and that union can never be broken. The instruction here is to remain in *communion* with Christ just as He remained in communion with the Father (Jn. 6:57).

"Abide in Me, and I in you" is a new principle which not only enables the born-again ones to "walk in newness of life," but to do so on the highest plane. Although this unique, intimate relationship with the Son of God is a revelation of God communicated explicitly only through the Apostle John, I cannot help but wonder if this is what the Spirit of God is saying also through the Apostle Paul in 1 Corinthians 3:12: "Now if any man build upon this foundation gold, silver and precious stones . . ."

Obviously "building gold" is intended to express the greatest thing the believer in Christ can do in his life and service. The standard of the greatest material riches is taken by the Spirit-directed writer as a symbol for the greatest spiritual value.

What then is building "gold"?

Could not the answer be that building "gold" means abiding in Christ? "Truly our fellowship is with the Father and with His Son Jesus Christ" (1 Jn. 1:2). Building gold is engaging in a direct, conscious and personal fellowship with God.

"Oh, the pure delight of a single hour
That before Thy throne I spend,
When I kneel in prayer and with Thee, my God,
I commune as friend with friend."

Robert Murray McCheyne (1813-1843), of Dundee, Scotland, whose life was such a passionate abandon to the love of Christ, said, "I ought to spend the best hours of the day in communion with God. It is my noblest and most fruitful employment."

Samuel Rutherford (1600-1661), the fair little man of Puritan days who has showed to many the "loveliness of Christ," said, "Ye must, I say, wait upon Him, and be often communing with Him."

Oswald Chambers (1874-1917) said, "The Christian worker is one who perpetually looks in the face of God and then goes forth to talk to people."

This little phrase "abide in Me" is filled with infinite potential because it literally opens the door for Christ to dwell in the believer. It is the same as if He said, "take heed that I may abide in you." It is difficult to conceive of any greater responsibility that the child of God has, than that of abiding in Christ.

"Abide in Me" is what Christ is saying to every child of God every day and every hour of his sojourn on earth. "It is as if He said, Think as I think; feel as I feel; will as I will; choose as I choose. Pursue My goals, use My means, rely on Me, entirely on Me. Let My wisdom be your wisdom—My righteousness your righteousness—My strength your strength. Come out of yourself. Come out of your limitations. Come into Me." (*John Brown,* 1722-1787, revised)

No Fruit . . . Nothing

"*As the branch cannot bear fruit of itself, except it abide in the vine*"—To abide in the vine is for the branch the one absolute condition of life and fruit. It has no life of its own.

"*No more can ye, except ye abide in Me*"—The believer who neglects to "abide" in Christ is like the branch trying to operate on its own: *nothing* without Him; *everything* by communion with Him. This is fulfilled, in the case of the branch, in organic oneness; in the experience of the believers, in spiritual oneness.

"*For without Me ye can do nothing*" our Lord declared. He did not say, "without Me you can do only half as much, or do just a little." He said emphatically, "Without Me you can do nothing." You can start nothing for Him and you can accomplish nothing for Him on your own. Often when a Christian awakens to the bleak state of barrenness in his life, he begins to be very active; he runs hither and thither; he gets on a number of committees; he wants to make up the years that the locusts have taken (Joel 2:25). But all this is done in the energy of the flesh; it has no substance in the sight of God. Usually in such activities the motives are wrong and usually there is no Christ in them.

When you are very busy in the service of the Lord, stop and consider if perhaps you may be actually producing *nothing*.

This is probably the most difficult spiritual truth to put across. Blessed are they whose hearts have been prepared to receive it, whose ears have been opened, and whose eyes see clearly that unless Christ is "formed" within and lives His life in us, that our big religious activities may be just so much "wood, hay and stubble" (1 Cor. 3:12).

Fruit . . . More Fruit . . . Much Fruit

"He that abideth in Me, and I in him, the same bringeth forth much fruit"—Get the sap flowing freely into the branch and there will be "much fruit." Let the believer take care to abide in Christ—live in uninterrupted fellowship with Him—and the supernatural life of Christ will rise and flow, and quietly there will come the abundant life and the fruitful service.

"Thou art the Vine,
And I, O Lord, am a branch of Thine;
And day by day from Thee
New life flows into me.
Naught have I of my own,
But all my strength
Is drawn from Thee alone."

-E. H. Divall

The Secret of Abiding in Christ

The secret for a life of abiding in Christ is disclosed in John 15:7: *"If ye abide in Me, and My words abide in you."* Having the word of God in the mind and heart—readily accessible—is the sure means of abiding in Christ.

Get a firm hold of this transforming truth!

The words of Christ, dwelling richly in the believer, become the food for holy thoughts, holy aspirations, holy purposes—yea, a holy life.

Follow closely. The disciple who is abiding in Christ and has the word of Christ abiding in him, will not begin by *acting*, but simply by *asking*: "Ye shall ask what ye will, and it shall be done unto you" (Jn. 15:7). The believer realizes that it is the divine strength, obtained through abiding in Christ, that he must depend on.

"Let that therefore abide in you which ye have heard from the beginning" (1 Jn. 2:24)—The message of salvation was first proclaimed, not in the words of men, but in the words of God. Now, let that word "abide" in you, and it will produce fruit for the glory of God. God's word is our most substantial possession, and without it, we blow around like a dandelion gone to seed.

"If that which ye have heard from the beginning remain in you, ye shall also continue in the Son, and in the Father" (1 Jn. 2:24). For some reason, the translators rendered John's favorite word "meno" in three different ways in this one verse—"abide," "remain" and "continue,"—thereby losing the emphasis intended by that repetition. Here is a paraphrase of that verse: Let the glorious truth, which you have heard from the beginning *abide* in you; if you do indeed feed upon that word and let it *abide* in you, you shall also *abide* in the Son and in the Father.

In this way, you will be living in communion with the Son and with the Father, and the supernatural life of God will be manifest in all your life and service.

When people ask me why I memorize Scripture, this glorious truth comes to mind at once, and I usually reply by saying, "I memorize Scripture because it helps me—enables me—to abide in Christ."

And *Jon McKeene*, Connecticut, says the same thing: "I've been saved just over ten years ago, and on looking back, my life for Christ has been fruitless. While reading the Scriptures, I read John 15:7, and it hit me like never before; the key to fruitfulness is memorizing the word."

> *"I'm only a little Branch, I live by a life not mine,*
> *For the sap that flows through my tendrils small*
> *Is the life-blood of the Vine."*

18

Overflowing

There is yet one more great benefit and blessing that comes with memorizing Scripture that I must mention. It is the filling with the Holy Spirit.

A life that is filled with the Spirit is one that is overflowing with the joy and blessing of the Lord. A young Christian girl once prayed, "O Lord, I can't hold much, but I can overflow a lot." And *Col. F. J. Miles* used to say, "It's the overflow of the cup that blesses other lives."

Have you ever been filled with the Holy Spirit? Are you now filled with the Holy Spirit? When does it occur? What brings it about?

Let us consider a few Scriptures on this important subject.

A person is "born of the Spirit" (Jn. 3:6), *indwelt* by the Spirit (1 Cor. 6:19), *baptized* and *sealed* by the Spirit (1 Cor. 12:13; Eph. 4:30). This work of the Spirit is accomplished once only in the life of the believer in Christ. The filling by the Holy Spirit, however, is a continuous process—repeated again and again.

Believers are commanded to be filled with the Spirit: "And be not drunk with wine wherein is excess;

but be filled with the Spirit" (Eph. 5:18). This is in the present tense, and means literally, *"keep on being filled with the Spirit."* The filling with the Holy Spirit is simply the unhindered control of a believer's life by the Holy Spirit, so He can fully bless the life for the glory of God and for its own enrichment. Filling with the Spirit is the normal work of God in the life of every believer who is growing in grace and submitting to the will of God.

Every Christian possesses the Holy Spirit, but it is only the Spirit-filled believer that is possessed by the Holy Spirit. Being filled with the Holy Spirit is not a matter of having more of the Spirit, but rather allowing the Holy Spirit to have more and more of the believer.

Now coming back to the Scripture quoted above: "Be not drunk with wine wherein is excess." The word for "excess" means "riot," "dissipation," "debauchery." The word is not adverbial in character telling us how much of the intoxicant a person should imbibe, but rather it is an adjective describing the nature of the intoxicant. It would read, therefore, "Be not drunk with wine wherein is riot."

Lewis Sperry Chafer points out that in the New Testament the effect of strong drink is placed over against the Spirit-filled life three times (Lu. 1:15; Acts 2:12-21; Eph. 5:18). "As strong drink stimulates the physical forces and men are prone to turn to it for help over the difficult places," he states, "so the child of God, facing an impossible responsibility of a heavenly walk and service, is directed to the Spirit as the source of all sufficiency."

Now the big question is *how* may a Christian be filled with the Spirit?

I believe that we will find a clear answer to this important question by comparing two Scriptures: In

Ephesians 5:18, we have noted that Paul writes, "Be filled with the Spirit." Then, in writing to the Colossians in a similar context to that of Ephesians 5:18-22, Paul says, "Let the word of Christ dwell in you richly in all wisdom; teaching and admonishing one another in psalms and hymns and spiritual songs, singing with grace in your hearts to the Lord" (3:16).

To the Ephesians Paul said, "Be filled with the Spirit." To the Colossians Paul says in almost an identical context, "Let the word of Christ dwell in you richly." The inescapable conclusion is that being filled with the Spirit and being filled with the word of God, though not synonymous, are absolutely *inseparable.* A person cannot really be filled with the Spirit who does not have the word of God filling his mind and heart continually.

When you are experiencing peace like a river and joy unspeakable and full of glory, and you want to sing and tell about it, you are actually being filled by the Spirit, and this comes as a result of being filled by the word of God. The filling with the Spirit is a solid, abiding reality, whether you are alone or whether you are with others. It is something that you can enjoy day after day. It is not just an occasional experience stimulated by feelings and primed by emotional group therapy.

This is so exceedingly important! This is one reason why we are in this ministry of encouraging and helping people to memorize Scripture systematically. "Thy words were found, and I did eat them," Jeremiah said, "and Thy word was unto me the joy and rejoicing of my heart" (15:16).

The Scripture which commands the filling by the Spirit is followed by five participles (two of them go together) which describe four very distinctive qualities of life which characterize the believer who is filled with the Spirit (Eph. 5:18-22).

Consider them carefully.

Speaking to yourselves in psalms and hymns and spiritual songs." A better rendering here is "speaking among yourselves." The saints who are filled with the Spirit are exhorted to edify one another by speaking intelligibly, using psalms and hymns and spiritual songs (1 Cor. 14:26). What psalms are they to use? Someone says, "Those in the Bible." We are prompted to say, "Well, yes, but you can use even better those psalms which have been stored up in the heart through diligent memorization." This is the point that *Carole Lewis,* Tennessee, wanted to make when she wrote: "The wonderful thing about hiding the Scriptures in your heart is that they are always there when you need them." We might add the fact they are there also for the Holy Spirit to use in our lives in those situations when we may not be keenly aware of our acute need.

"Singing and making melody in your heart to the Lord." As the word dwells richly in the heart and abounds, the Spirit of God fills the heart, and the believer is rejoicing and singing praises unto the Lord. This is "joy unspeakable and full of glory" (1 Pet. 1:8). This is joy celestial and it's just what the Lord meant when He said, "These things have I spoken unto you, that My joy might remain in you, and that your joy might be full" (Jn. 15:11).

"Giving thanks always for all things." Another quality of the Spirit-filled life is the ability to give thanks to God, not only for the blessings He bestows, but for *all* the experiences of life—the triumphs and the defeats, the joys and the sorrows—which our heavenly Father providentially brings into our lives. It is indeed His will that we give thanks "in everything" (1 Thess. 5:18).

"Submitting yourselves one to another." There is always to be a happy harmony in the home and in the

fellowship of God's people working together. No rivalry, no pride, no self-exaltation. Each is to submit himself voluntarily for the Lord's sake. Obviously such harmony and fellowship will not exist unless each believer is continually feeding on the word and submitting himself to the will of God.

Another Scripture that deals specifically with the filling by the Holy Spirit is John 7:38-39: "He that believeth on Me, as the Scripture hath said, out of his belly shall flow rivers of living water. (But this spake He of the Spirit, which they that believe on Him should receive: for the Holy Ghost was not yet given; because that Jesus was not yet glorified.)"

Out of the innermost being of the believer the "living water" shall continually rise and overflow. This is probably the meaning of our Lord's word to the woman of Samaria: "But whosoever drinketh of the water that I shall give him shall never thirst; but the water that I shall give him shall be in him a well of water springing up into everlasting life" (Jn. 4:14).

The operations of the Holy Spirit described in John 7:38-39 are wonderful to contemplate. We list four things following an outline suggested by C. H. *Spurgeon:*

This is to be an *inward* work; the rivers of living water are to flow from the heart of the believer.

It is a *life-giving* work. The believer is the instrument in which the divine life is communicated to others.

See how *spontaneous* it is. No pumping is required. The Christian just goes about flooding the world with blessing, and instead of attracting attention to himself, it may well be that he himself is unconscious of what he is effecting.

And this is to be *perpetual,*—not like intermittent springs which burst forth and flow in torrents, and then cease,—but it is to be an everyday outgushing! "In summer and winter, by day and by night, wherever the believer is, he shall be a blessing. As he breathes, he shall breathe benedictions; as he thinks, his mind shall be devising generous things; and when he acts, his acts shall be as though the hand of God were working by the hand of man."

Rivers of living water shall overflow from his innermost being. Someone has calculated that there flows continually out of the mouth of the great Congo River in Africa one million cubic feet of water, not per day, not per hour, not per minute, not per second, but *per every half second!* Think of it. And out of the innermost being of the believer shall flow not one Congo but many Congos of living water—yea, an inconceivable plenitude of spiritual power and blessing.

And that's why we are always memorizing Scripture so that we can meditate therein night and day. The Holy Spirit takes the word in our hearts and opens the springs of "living water" that will overflow to the thirsty multitudes.

19

Translations

In the last forty years, there has been an average of just about one new English translation of the Bible per year. The many translations present something of a problem, but not one that is insurmountable.

The Bible is absolutely trustworthy.

It is not our intention to condemn any translation. Probably all of the translators began their work with a sincere desire to make the Scriptures more understandable. Some have succeeded more than others. Those with certain biases seek to promote their beliefs in their translations wherever possible.

We must recognize that no translation of the holy Scriptures is perfect. There are small mistakes, ambiguities, and imperfections even in the very best translations, for the work of the translators is not inspired. Furthermore, the English language—like any other modern language—changes, and as time progresses, revisions become necessary.

In this one chapter we essentially want to consider certain principles involved in Bible translation and how those principles affect the choices of a translation for memorization.

Divine Inspiration of the Original Scriptures

The Bible was produced over a period of more than fifteen centuries by a great variety of human writers, ranging from scholars to fishermen. It was given originally in three different languages. The bulk of the Old Testament came in Hebrew, with four passages in Aramaic. The New Testament was written in Greek, which was the universal language in the time of Christ's sojourn on earth.

The Bible is a *miracle* Book. The original writings (often referred to as autographs) of the Scriptures came by direct inspiration of God, and are completely without error. God did not use just any human instrument that came along. He prepared each human author beforehand, which included the background, the training, the personality and the writing style. The net result was the Bible—an inspired record of divine revelation in the exact words of God, but in the language, literary style and personality of the human authors.

Each book in the Bible bears the unmistakable impress of the individual human author, yet each one wrote only as he was "moved"—borne along—by the Holy Spirit (2 Pet. 1:21). Just as the incarnate Word, the Lord Jesus Christ, was subject to the weaknesses and limitations of humanity, yet remained absolutely perfect, so the written word is a revelation of God couched in the feeble symbolism of human speech, but is nevertheless pure, perfect and inerrant. The words of the Lord are not affected in their value by the medium through which they came.

"All Scripture is given by inspiration of God" (2 Tim. 3:16). The word "inspiration" in the King James Version is a little ambiguous. The original Greek word is *theopneustos*, and as B. B. *Warfield*, the prince of exegetes and theologians, explains, "It has nothing to say of *inspiring* or *inspiration*: it speaks only of a 'spiring' or 'spiration.' What it says of Scripture is not that it is 'breathed into by God' or is the product of divine inbreathing into its human authors, but that it is breathed *out* by God— 'God-breathed,' —the product of the creative breath of God. In a word, what is declared by this fundamental passage is simply that the Scriptures are a divine product, without any indication of how God has operated in producing them."

Divine inspiration of the Scriptures in the original languages covers not only "concepts" or thoughts, but reaches down to the very exact choice of the words used (1 Cor. 2:13). "Thoughts are wedded to words," one scholar notes, "as necessarily as soul is to body." Otherwise we might as well speak of a "tune without notes, or a sum without figures." The theory that only thoughts came from God is unintelligible and illogical. *Shakespeare*, in speaking about prayer in *Hamlet*, said "Words without thoughts never to heaven go." In reversing his statement we believe that thoughts without words never from heaven came. The thoughts and the words are inseparable, and both are equally inspired of God, but it is the words that dictate the thoughts.

This is a fundamental doctrine and is known as the *verbal, plenary inspiration* of the Scriptures. It means that the Holy Spirit guided in the exact choice of the words (*verbal*) used in the original writings, and that this inspiration extends to every portion of the Bible (*plenary*), from Latin, *plenus*, meaning "full."

We are not asked to believe in the supernatural inspiration of the copyist, or the translator or the interpreter, where superficial errors may exist, but we are asked to believe that the originals, as written by the prophets and apostles, were absolutely perfect, and free from any error because they came from God.

They represent God. They speak for God. They are His revelation in human language, and God Himself has "magnified" His word above all His name (Ps. 138: 2).

The words of Scripture come to us with a *present* inspiration. Our Lord said, "The words that I speak unto you, they are spirit, and they are life" (Jn. 6:63). This Book is not just ink and paper. In it are thoughts that breathe and words that pierce. *Martin Luther* said of the Bible, "This book is alive; it speaks to me. It has legs; it runs after me. It has hands; it lays hold of me."

Joseph Parker (1830-1902), whose commentary, *The People's Bible,* has been a window in Bible understanding for many believers, has been credited with sitting in his study for lengthy periods of time, tapping an open Bible with his fingers and saying, "This is history—exhausts all history! This is poetry—exhausts all poetry! This is truth—exhausts all truth!"

The Bible Claims of Divine Inspiration

There are those who teach that the Bible represents man's search or groping after God, and that the words in it are simply the best insights of godly people during those many years. Those who hold such a view must also hold open, as indeed they do, the possibility that the writers of the Scriptures were wrong, that their stories may be fiction and that their ideas and thoughts may be false.

But the Scriptures do not represent the speculations of men. They are a record of a divine, verbal revelation. They "proceed out of the mouth of the Lord" (Deut. 8:3). They are the outgoing, the outbreathing of God (Isa. 55:11). More than 2,600 times in the Old Testament, the writers claim to be giving, not their own words, but the words of God. This is expressed in statements such as: "Hear the word of the Lord . . . The word of the Lord came unto . . . Thus saith the Lord." They knew that they were communicating the messages of God to man.

In the New Testament, we see how the Lord Jesus Christ quoted the words of the Old Testament as being authentic. The Apostles similarly attested to the divine origin of the Scriptures. The Apostle Paul said to the Thessalonians, "When ye received the word of God which ye heard of us, ye received it not as the word of men, but as it is in truth the word of God, which effectually worketh also in you that believe" (1 Thess. 2:13).

Furthermore, there are scores of passages in the Bible which proclaim the excellence and divine origin of the Scriptures. "The words of the Lord are pure words: as silver tried in a furnace of earth, purified seven times" (Ps. 12:6). Again, "Thy word is very pure: therefore Thy servant loveth it" (Ps. 119:140). And again, "The law of the Lord is perfect... The testimony of the Lord is sure... The statutes of the Lord are right ... The commandment of the Lord is pure ... The judgments of the Lord are true and righteous altogether" (Ps. 19:7-9).

What God revealed many years ago, He speaks to us now, "for He will not call back His words" (Isa. 31: 2). His word "is forever settled in heaven" (Ps. 119:89).

"Thy word is true from the beginning: and every one of Thy righteous judgments endureth forever" (Ps. 119:160). "The grass withereth, the flower fadeth: but the word of our God shall stand forever" (Isa. 40: 8). "For whatsoever things were written aforetime were written for our learning, that we through patience and comfort of the Scriptures might have hope" (Rom. 15:4).

Our Lord declared, "Heaven and earth shall pass away, but My words shall not pass away" (Matt. 24:35).

The Early English Translations

Portions of the Bible were translated into English by *The Venerable Bede* (672-735) and by *King Alfred the Great* (849-901). The first distinguishing achievement in English translation was the work of those who were associated with *John Wycliffe* (1320-1384).

William Tyndale (1494-1536) was the first to translate into English the New Testament directly from the Greek. He used the Erasmus Greek New Testament and consulted the Latin translation of Erasmus, as well as Luther's German text and the Latin Vulgate. He translated into English a considerable portion of the Old Testament, using the Masoretic text, but he was burned at the stake before he could complete it. His dying prayer was that God would open the eyes of the king of England.

Tyndale, whose style and spirit were the foundation for the King James Version, wrote, "I call God to record against the day we shall appear before our Lord Jesus Christ to give reckoning of our doings that I never altered one syllable of God's Word against my conscience, nor would I this day, if all that is in the earth— whether it be honor, pleasure or riches—might be given me."

The first translation into English of the complete Bible was that of *Myles Coverdale*. It was published in 1535. In his preface, Coverdale wrote concerning the value of differing translations as follows: "Let this present translation be no prejudice to the other that out of the Greek have been translated afore, or shall be hereafter. For if thou open thine eyes and consider well the gift of the Holy Spirit, thou shalt see that one translation declareth, openeth and illustrateth another, and that in many cases one is a plain commentary unto another." This reminds us of a similar word spoken by *St. Augustine* (354-430) when referring to the varied

Latin translations of his day: "The variety of translations is profitable for the finding out of the sense of the Scriptures." The Body of Christ today would be much more edified if this kind of attitude prevailed among the followers of the different translations.

The *Thomas Matthew* translation appeared in 1537. (This was actually the work of *John Rogers*, one of Tyndale's companions.) Then came *The Taverner's Bible* in 1539, and *The Great Bible* (so called because of its large size) in 1539, which was prepared by *Myles Coverdale* at the request of *Thomas Cromwell*. It was generally referred to as *Cromwell's Bible*.

There were no new English translations until 1560 when the *Geneva Bible* appeared.

In the five-year reign of *Queen Mary Tudor—Bloody Mary—*(1516-1558), Bibles were taken from the churches, and many protestants suffered martyrdom. Some fled to the continent. A group of such under the leadership of *William Whittingham* prepared the *"Geneva Bible"*. Verse divisions were employed for the first time throughout the entire Bible. The Geneva Bible was dedicated to Queen Elizabeth, and achieved "a dominant popularity" in the period 1570-1620. It made an enormous contribution to the *King James Bible* and is the source of many of the Biblical allusions in Shakespeare.

The Bishop's Bible first appeared in 1568, with a careful revision in 1572. The work was done by bishops under the direction of *Matthew Parker*, the Archbishop of Canterbury. The 1572 edition influenced the translators of the *King James Version* in considerable measure.

The Authorized Version

In 1604, King James I appointed fifty-four learned men for the work of a new translation of the Bible. The completed translation was published in 1611, and became known as the *Authorized Version*. It soon began to be known also as the *King James Bible*. They adopted the reliable Hebrew Masoretic Text for their Old Testament translation.

The King James translators worked from the earliest printed texts (often identified as the Textus Receptus or the Received Text). Though unknown to those who compiled the early printed texts, these printed texts reflected a form of text which is found in a large majority of the Greek manuscripts which survive today. The text found in the majority of the Greek manuscripts is often referred to today as the Majority Text. "A strong case can be made that all translations ought to follow the Majority Text as the King James Version basically does" (*Zane C. Hodges*).

The King James translators looked favorably upon the earlier English translations. Much of their text came from the other translations, particularly that of Tyndale, Coverdale and the Geneva Bible. About ninety percent of the language of the New Testament, we are told, was the language of Tyndale, and everywhere was the influence of "that consummate master of rhythmical prose," Myles Coverdale. They never designed "to make a completely new translation, or to change a bad one into a good one," but their aim was "to make a good one better, or out of many good ones, one principal good one." This is stated by Miles Smith in his long introduction, on behalf of the Translation Committee, to the 1611 edition of the *King James Bible*.

They were unhurried in their task. They consulted translators in various other languages. They followed meticulously the principle of a word-for-word translation. When the original text seemed unclear, they took account of the diversity of meaning in the margin. Words that were added for a more smooth reading were placed in italics or brackets.

The language of the Authorized Version was distinctive. Its simple, majestic and rhythmic style, its directness and force of utterance became the model in diction, cadence and dignity of the English writers. Its phrasing is woven into some of our finest English literature.

The Authorized Version immediately replaced the Bishop's Bible in the churches, and within fifty years of its publication date, it became the dominant translation in the English language. It has held this position now for over three hundred and eighty years, although some of the modern translations are now gaining ascendancy.

The Revisions

There were three minor revisions of the King James Bible along the way, and in 1769 there was a major revision which involved some 24,000 changes, according to the English Bible Society in London. The King James Version used today is not the 1611 edition but the 1769 revision. The original 1611 edition may be obtained from Thomas Nelson Publishing, Nashville Tennessee.

In 1881, the *English Revised Version* was published after many stormy debates among the translators. The new translation departed considerably from the Textus Receptus. It was based on the Westcott and Hort's New Testament Greek text, which depended heavily on much earlier Vaticanus and Sinaiticus Greek manuscripts. Although the argument from "earliest manuscripts" can be made in favor of better reliability, it is a well-established principle in textual research that the oldest manuscripts do not always have the best text.

The *American Standard Version* of 1901, the *Revised Standard Version* of 1952, and the *New American Standard*

Bible of 1971 followed closely the English Revised Version of 1881. Although these translations largely represent a departure from the Textus Receptus Greek text of all the earlier English translations, they are careful word-for-word translations, and we can find many illuminating renderings in them, particularly in the Old Testament where the reliable Hebrew Masoretic text was used as the basis for translation.

In 1959 the *Berkeley Bible* appeared. It is a translation by Gerrit Verkuyl.

The *New International Version* (NIV) was published in 1978. It is not a revision but a new translation. In translating the New Testament, they adopted an "eclectic" Greek text, which means that their source was a selection from various Greek texts. It was at once endorsed by some leading evangelicals.

NIV is a good translation but it has some problems. In the preface to NIV we read that "the first concern of the translators has been the accuracy of the translation and its fidelity to the *thought* of the biblical writers" (italics mine). Should not their concern have been a fidelity to the *words* of the biblical writers? The translators appear to be conveying the idea that their objective was a thought-for-thought translation instead of a complete equivalence, word-for-word translation.

However, NIV is a major effort at Bible translation. Many deep insights can be gained from it, especially in the study where it can be compared with other translations and checked with the original languages themselves.

The *New King James Version* was first published in 1982 after seven years of diligent work. As in the case of the King James translators, it was not their purpose "to make a new translation . . . but to make a good one better." It is a word-for-word translation in tune with the old King James. The revision is based on the Textus

Receptus Greek text in the New Testament and the Masoretic text in the Old Testament as was the King James of 1611.

Although it has been on the market only nine years, it is receiving positive marks in a variety of churches and denominations. The consensus of many leading evangelicals is that the New King James retains the beauty of the original King James while removing its few imperfections and archaisms. It is basically the same authoritative book that has been used for centuries.

The Thought-for-Thought Principle

In the twentieth century a new phenomenon in Bible translation appeared. It is generally identified as thought-for-thought translation, or what is often called "dynamic equivalence." Instead of a word-for-word translation, as in almost all of the previous English versions, the aim here is to capture the thrust and meaning of the original inspired words, and express it in words that are easy to read and understand. Such a translation, we are told, really communicates in today's English.

But we ask at once, what does such a translation communicate? Is it indeed the exact message of God or is it at least in part the message of what the translator honestly *thinks* God intended to say? What we want from a translator is the word from God. We are not interested in what *he* thinks the original words should mean. We want to be assured that the translation represents fairly what God said. *Dr. James H. Brooks,* a Presbyterian pastor in St. Louis for many years, used to say about Exodus 4:10-12, "It is not 'I will be with thy mind and teach thee what thou shalt think,' but 'I will be with thy mouth and teach thee what thou shalt say,' because while it does not much matter what Moses thought, it *does* matter what he actually said."

154

The principle of "dynamic equivalence" or a "thought-for-thought" translation sounds very promising and has gained wide acceptance in our day. The actual words are considered to be less important than

ORIGIN and GROWTH of the ENGLISH BIBLE — 4220

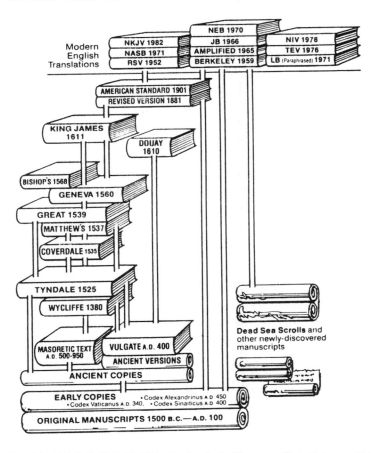

Copyright 1983 B. B. Kirkbride Bible Co., Inc. in the Thompson Chain-Reference Bible. Used by permission.

the thoughts or ideas which they convey. But such an approach is flawed at the very outset because we do not have the thoughts of any of the Bible writers. C. H. Spurgeon is right: "If God had spoken to us by some way in which His thoughts and meaning were infallible, but His words were questionable or unimportant, we should have been more puzzled than edified." The thought-for-thought principle espouses a noble goal, but it is untenable because in effect it begins and ends with the thoughts of the translator.

We do not have the thoughts of the Bible writers, as such, but we do have their words. The Lord Jesus said, "I have given them Thy word" (Jn. 17:14). Translation, therefore, has to deal with the God-inspired words. The translator should aim at formal or complete equivalence as nearly as the science of language translation allows. He must always strive for accuracy. Every word must be carefully taken into account. In addition to the vocabulary, the grammar, the form and the syntax must be carefully observed. This is the normal, traditional principle of translation whether applied to the Scriptures or to any other work of literature. Serious problems are encountered in the process, but we are dealing with the holy word of God. Idioms, figures of speech, difficult words and sentence structure must be handled with unlimited respect. The care with which the sacred text is to be handled may be observed in the solemn warning of one rabbi to a scribe: "Take heed how thou doest thy work, for thy work is the work of heaven, lest thou drop or add a letter of the manuscript and so become a destroyer of the world."

A faithful translation will make sure that the reader is aware of any words which are added to the text. This is done in the traditional use of italics for words which are demanded or implied by the original language and context and for the "helper" words which are used to complete the sense of the text.

The issue here is far-reaching and one of vast proportions, because we are dealing with the eternal and inerrant words which God has given us. The divine revelation in the Bible is intended for all generations. In it we have exceedingly deep and profound truths, which are structured and charged with the infinite. Even the prophets whom God used in the writing of the Scriptures did not fully comprehend the message of God; and, therefore, "inquired and searched diligently" concerning the meaning of the things which "the Spirit of Christ that was in them did signify" (1 Pet. 1:10-12).

If we believe in *verbal inspiration*, then we must believe that the holy men of old, though using their own language and following their own convictions, were led by the Spirit of God to use words which were also the words of God. Every word of God is right and sure. Every word of God is true and righteous altogether.

The Thought-for-Thought Translations

These thought-for-thought translations (inclined to add, omit, or change the original words) began to appear at the turn of this century. One of the first ones was the *Weymouth* translation of the New Testament. It was done by *Richard F. Weymouth* (1822-1902), and was published in 1903, one year after his death.

The *Expanded Translation* of *Kenneth S. Wuest* came in the forties and fifties. *The Amplified Bible* was published in 1964, and there were several with liberal leanings such as the *Moffat*, the *Goodspeed*, the *Revised Standard Version* and the *Good News for Today*.

The New Testament translation by *J. B. Phillips* fascinated me exceedingly some twenty-five years ago. The richness of his renderings made me wonder why the King James translators and others missed all this wonderful truth. But alas, as I thumbed through the Greek Testament, I soon discovered that the King James translators were not the ones who missed what God said; instead, it was Mr. Phillips who elaborated on what God had spoken.

It was encouraging, however, to learn some years later that Mr. Phillips had a high regard for the truth of the sacred text and that it frightened him when he realized the extent of freedom he used in his first editions. "This passion of mine for communication," he is quoted as saying in his 1972 edition, "had led me sometimes into paraphrase and sometimes to interpolate clarifying remarks which are certainly not in the Greek."

It must also be said that the publishers of Weymouth's New Testament stated clearly "that his translation was not intended to supplant the versions then in general use, but to act as a compressed running commentary on them."

Mr. Kenneth S. Wuest spoke similarly in identifying his translation, "The expanded translation is not intended as a substitute for regular translations, but as a help in bringing out the meaning bound up in the original." In 1971 *The Living Bible* was published by the Tyndale House Publishers, but Dr. Kenneth Taylor, the author, stated clearly that it was a paraphrase. Many people have been helped by reading the paraphrase and then encouraged to read the literal translations.

In the last year or two, the translators of the so-called "easy Bibles" state that their aim was having a "translation in plain English that is as easy to read as the morning newspaper." This is an unfortunate comparison.

This process of simplification continues unabated at a frightening pace. The committee of one of these versions goes on to say, "We reject the concept of a word-for-word translation." One of the translators is quoted as saying further, "We had to take a stand on what each verse meant and explain it in clear and simple terms." This is a fearsome stand.

But the responsibility of the translator is not to "explain" but to render word for word what the original inspired text declares. Some small interpretations may be necessary in translating, but they should be held to the very minimum that the science of language translation requires. The translator should strive for the nearest approximation in words and concepts. He must scrupulously avoid adding words or thoughts not demanded by the text. He must ever minimize the insertion of his own humanity. His task is not to expand or to explain, but to translate. If an accurate and intelligible translation does not seem to communicate, we can trust the Holy Spirit to illuminate that in His own way and time.

The necessary explanations and the variant readings belong in the margin and footnotes. Further explaining is the task of the commentaries.

Amplification and paraphrases of the sacred text are acceptable and often prove helpful, so long as they are clearly identified as such.

The real problem is not that the "easy Bibles" now exist, but the fact that they at once seem to receive the endorsement from strong evangelical leaders and institutions. If the translation is endorsed by Dr. So-and-So and is recommended by such-and-such institution, then it must be good, they say. People generally are not in a position to know the difference. They follow the leaders. The faithful members do not exactly know why the pastor suddenly placed a different translation in the pew.

The acceptance of the "easy Bibles" by many sincere Christians is distressing! Within less than one century, we have turned 180 degrees from the word-for-word translation to a complete rejection of such translation!

In all fairness at least to the better of the thought-for-thought translations, we must recognize two things:

First, some of the "thought-for-thought" translations are in large measure a word-for-word translation. It seems that the translators of some of these versions felt that they had to resort to a thought-for-thought rendition where a word-for-word translation of the passages would be stilted and not easy to understand. Unfortunately, this is where interpolations, explanations and the thoughts of the translator are incorporated. These are often difficult to notice because most of these translators are doctrinally sound and their "explanations" do not jar the Christian reader.

Second, some of these translators never intended that we should abandon the literal word-for-word translations. They meant that their translations should be regarded as study helps as in the case of Weymouth, Wuest and others.

There is the strong tendency in the "easy Bibles" to explain everything and solve every problem at the risk of altering the intent in the original writings. We ought not to be surprised if we find problems in the Bible which we cannot solve. These are the words of the infinite God and we must not think that we can grasp the full meaning at once.

The Version for Memorizing

There is no perfect translation with a divine imprimatur on the title page. We simply recognize that in translating God's word a literal translation is preferable. The less insertion of the human element the better. Therefore, we recommend that you choose from among translations that rely most heavily on the word-for-word translation principle.

The use of italics for added words—as in the King James, the New King James and the American Standard—is helpful. Many people find the King James and the New King James easier to memorize because of the distinctive style of writing. The diction, the cadence, the poetic flow and the particular sentence structure contribute to that distinctiveness.

Finally, let us keep our attention on the primary issue—memorizing the word of God. Having chosen a reliable translation, let us so inscribe God's words upon our minds and hearts that it may truly be said of us: they "meditate" in God's words "day and night" (Ps. 1:2).

Let us once again become excited about memorizing the Scriptures. The translation explosion, though commendable in certain respects, has discouraged memorizing the living word in *any* translation. Let us not allow the dilemma of the many translations to deter us from the task. Think upon the instruction and power inherent in the Psalmist's testimony: "Thy word have I hid in my heart, that I might not sin against Thee" (Ps. 119:11). Prayerfully review the other chapters in this book and God bless you as you "lay up" His precious word in your mind and heart.

Forever Settled

Thank God for the Bible, the inerrant, infallible, eternal revelation of God. Though translations, with their small human imperfections and with the continuing changes in language, come and go, we may all joyfully exclaim with the Psalmist, "For ever, O Lord, Thy word is settled in heaven" (Ps. 119:89).

The Bible is the *Book of books*. The story of the dying Sir Walter Scott, the great English writer, is appropriate. As he was approaching death, Scott who possessed a great library, called to his son, "Bring me the book!" "Which book?" asked the son. Sir Walter Scott replied, "There is only *one* book; it is the Bible."

The Bible is such a book which man could not write if he would, because it is beyond his ability, nor would he write it if he could, because it condemns him.

Someone wrote a summary of that which makes the Bible the "world's most unique book": This Book, the word of God, contains "the state of man, the way of salvation, the doom of sinners, and the happiness of believers. Its doctrines are holy, its precepts are binding, its histories are truth, and its decisions are immutable. Read it to be wise, believe it to be safe, and practice it to be holy.

"It contains light to direct you, food to support you, and comfort to cheer you. It is the traveler's map, the pilgrim's staff, the pilot's compass, the soldier's sword, and the Christian's charter. Here paradise is restored, heaven opened, and the gates of hell disclosed. Christ is its grand object, our good its design, and the glory of God its end. It should fill the memory, rule the heart, and guide the feet.

"Read it slowly, frequently, prayerfully. It is a mine of wealth, a paradise of glory, and a river of pleasure. It is given in life, will be opened at the judgment, and be remembered forever. It involves the highest responsibility, will restore the greatest labor, and condemns all who trifle with its sacred contents."

Therefore, "I will delight myself in Thy statutes: I will not forget Thy word" (Ps. 119:16).